THE BEST FRIEND
I EVER HAD

For Melia & Roberta —
    This book is about friends
and don't flinch if I say I
consider you friends. If so, imagine
how proud I am. Enjoy the book.
It is interesting.

THE BEST FRIEND I EVER HAD

I EVER HAD

*Revelations about Ernest Hemingway
from those who knew him*

David Nuffer

To order additional copies of this book, contact:
Xlibris Corporation
1-888-795-4274
www.Xlibris.com
Orders@Xlibris.com
51746

CONTENTS

End Papers

To friends—the few of them that most of us
have—and to one in particular.

PREFACE

My Quest

One day in 1971, I found myself walking down the aisles of the tiny Ocean Beach library in San Diego, California, looking for Hemingway's *For Whom the Bell Tolls*. I had never read it, and it was about time; after all, I was 39. I had read Hemingway before in high school and college, and his *Death in the Afternoon* triggered a lifelong interest in bullfighting. But I had stopped too soon.

For Whom the Bell Tolls began a new avocation. Avocations can lead to casual obsessions, and I was hooked. "Hemania" might be a word to describe my interest in Hemingway although I don't consider myself manic.

I have now read nearly every biography of the author—and they are a multitude—and much more. At home, my Hemingway collection consists of the following:

* Two hundred and fifty-two books, including first editions of most of Hemingway's books
* The complete 26-edition package of *Ken*, a leftist magazine from the late '30s, 14 of which carry articles by Hemingway about the Spanish Civil War
* Three copies of the Sunday, March 1, 1992, edition of the *Toronto Star*, which includes the lost Hemingway stories, written by him when he worked for the paper in 1922
* Twenty-five editions of the *Lost Generation Journal*, now defunct
* Hundreds of other magazines, magazine articles, and newspaper clippings

* Twenty-one videos, cassettes, and records, including "On the American Dead in Spain," an under-the-counter recording of the speech Hemingway wrote in Cuba in 1947 for a reunion of the Lincoln Battalion, which was composed of Americans who had volunteered for the Spanish Civil War
* Letters, posters and other things

At least a billion words have been written by or about Hemingway. Nearly 24 million words reside under my roof alone. He lived 61 years and 183 days, or 538,752 hours. Just loosely, this means that roughly 2,000 words per hour have been written about him for every hour of his life. And more are written every day. This is pure sophistry of course, but no matter how you categorize the man, it is no wonder he is a legend.

Conferences

From 1985 to 1994, I attended a number of conferences centered on Ernest Hemingway. It was at these that I first rubbed shoulders with academe, but few of the college professors turned to talk to me. I was merely a fan. I hold the academics in great respect because accuracy is one of their principles. I listened well and learned much.

Some of these conferences are discussed in more depth later in this book, but here's a summary:

* Hemingway: A Moveable Feast, the Third Annual Literary Seminar sponsored by the Council for Florida Libraries, Key West, Florida, January 10-13, 1985
* Hemingway in Idaho Conference, the Boise State University Hemingway Western Studies Center, Sun Valley, Idaho, June 9-11, 1989
* Ernest Hemingway at the Kennedy, the Fourth International Hemingway Conference, July 7-11, 1990, John F. Kennedy Library, Boston, Massachusetts, 10th anniversary of the formation of the Hemingway Society
* Michigan Hemingway Society Conference, Petoskey, Michigan, October 1991
* Hemingway/Fitzgerald International Conference, Paris, France, July 3-8, 1994
* Second Annual Ernest Hemingway Festival, Sun Valley, Idaho, September 28-October 1, 2006

The Places

I've been to about 165 Hemingway-related sites in Canada, Cuba, Europe, and the United States, including 15 homes or apartments where he lived and/or wrote and the rooms where he was born and died. What and where are listed in END PAPERS, Item Five, A Personal Postscript.

So with all this tucked away in my memory, paper, and computer files, I took on the pleasant task of writing about Ernest Hemingway and people who knew him.

Remember, of course, that I am an advocate. I am not alone, as this book attests.

In a sense, this book is autobiographical because it deals with my interactions with Hemingway's friends and relatives featured here. I hope this does not distract from the insights provided by those interviewed.

My goal here has been to add to the lore of hidden anecdotes and observations already published. As Hemingway's protagonist Nick Adams says in the movie *Hemingway's Adventures of a Young Man*, "There's something started in me that I've got to finish."

ACKNOWLEDGMENTS

My thanks to those crucial to this writing: my forbearing wife, Mary, who patiently, and with a smile, joined me in my pilgrimage across the world in pursuit of the spirit and essence of Ernest Hemingway; Walter Houk and his lovely, accepting wife, Nita, who befriended me and helped immeasurably in the making of this book; Donna Kimbell, sister of Tillie Arnold, and her husband, Virgil, who helped me navigate through the last years of Tillie and her death; Tally Larrick, wife of a friend, who arranged my meeting with her cousin's husband, Patrick Hemingway; Shannon Besoyan and Bill Smallwood of Sun Valley, Idaho, who strengthened my ties with Hemingway's last home, nearby Ketchum; Sun Valley Resort for granting me the use of three of its archival photos of Hemingway and friends; Professor Jim Brasch, who researched and wrote the landmark book about Hemingway's library at the Finca Vigia outside Havana; Allan Fesmire, old Hemingway buddy from several Hemingway Society meetings; Earlie Joe Parker, writer and critic, who helped me improve on the title of this book and the preface and introduction; Marie Carey and Valerie Lemke, who were always encouraging; Kerry Tucker, a longtime partner, pal, and supporter; and talented friends from my public relations agency, Bill Trumpfheller, Mary Moreno, Tanya Johnson, Elena Ortuno, Janet Elk, webmaster, and Michelle Livermore, graphic design genius.

Special plaudits go to John Mann, my talented editor and friend, and, again, Walter Houk.

I must sincerely and gratefully acknowledge the stars of this book, who, to my knowledge, have joined Hemingway after my contacts with them: Nita Houk, Jose Garate, Tillie Arnold, Betty Bruce, Frank Aldrich, Dr. Ed Rynearson, Mary Hemingway, Herb Saul, and William Johnson.

And since I know I must have forgotten someone, I want you to know, I acknowledge you too.

INTRODUCTION

Let's Tell It Like It Is

He was seemingly human. He had a conventional birth and his death, while not conventional, was a human choice.

He was born into a middle-class family in a Chicago suburb with wide, shaded streets and no slum. He was the older of two boys, and he had four sisters. His father was a doctor, and his mother was a talented singer. Until he graduated from high school, his life was dominated by the upcountry woods and waters of Michigan. With the guidance of his father, he developed a love of hunting and fishing, camping and adventure. There was nothing unusual about this; it was a legacy of earlier days of survival in pioneer America. Heavy drinking was another legacy; the ability to "hold your liquor well" made you more of a man.

At three years old, when asked what he was afraid of, he replied, "'Fraid o' nothing." Perhaps this "simple declarative sentence" laid the parameters for a life to come.

The seeds of becoming something beyond human were sown in Upper Michigan, and the first shoots on the stem appeared when he was a cub reporter for the *Kansas City Star*. From then on, he was not one who could be called "conventional."

In his seven-month tenure there (October 1917 to April 1918), he showed a desire and a talent for being where danger was and where he could get firsthand knowledge of events as they happened. Ted Brumback, his pal there and a fellow cub reporter, wrote that Hemingway had a "boundless energy" and uncommon courage. When he and Ted decided to join the Red Cross ambulance corps in Italy, Ted wrote that Hemingway was "delirious with excitement." And when they arrived in Paris on the first leg of the trip, he insisted that they drive to where German shells were at that moment falling on Paris.

From Italy on, Hemingway's life became a "high on the wild" adventure, to use the title of a book written about him by his Ketchum friend, Lloyd "Pappy" Arnold. He was one of life's great warriors in the last century. He was a risk taker supreme. He put himself in the line of fire in three wars, first as an ambulance driver in Italy where he was injured saving a comrade and then as a journalist in the Spanish Civil War and World War II. Early on in that war, he engaged in a perilous, clandestine search for German submarines prowling Gulf and Atlantic waters off the north coast of Cuba. One of his fictional characters spoke of those who lived life "all the way up." Who can dispute that this was exactly the way Hemingway lived his life?

There is no end to the list of adjectives that have been used to describe Hemingway. The best condensed version is in the foreword to Carlos Baker's official biography, *Ernest Hemingway: A Life Story*. What other man or woman in the last century merited such descriptive attention?

Here is what a few observers, admittedly admirers, have had to say:

> "Archibald MacLeish, a friend from the 1920s in Paris, declared that he had known only two men in his life who could empty the air from a room simply by entering it: Franklin Delano Roosevelt and Ernest Hemingway. In large part, Hemingway simply could not stop people from talking about him."
>
> —Scott Donaldson, *Hemingway vs. Fitzgerald*

> "I mourn for Hemingway. He could be mean as cat piss and as sweet as a ministering angel. It's hard to think that so much vitality, vanity, unflagging zest, eagerness to excel in everything, willingness to learn and study and finally teach everything, ability to participate in other people's lives—that all this should simply vanish."
>
> —Malcolm Cowley, biographer,
> five days after Hemingway's death

> "When he enjoyed life . . . he enjoyed it to the fullest. And he had the gift of being able to impart his pleasure and enthusiasm to those around him . . . He tended to exaggerate greatly, and mostly this was fun and enhanced every activity . . . He had the most inquiring mind of anyone I've ever met. Although his knowledge was vast and diverse, he constantly deferred to those around him, asking their

opinion and valuing the answer . . . Trust was a quality he valued most in those surrounding him."
> —Valerie Hemingway, widow of Hemingway's third son, Gregory, *Running with the Bulls: My Years with the Hemingways.*

"He enjoyed the land, the sea, great ideas and small ones too, plus sports, literature and everyone who plied an honest trade. He let nothing interfere with his work, not even drink."
> —Valerie Hemingway, *Smithsonian*, August 2007

"[He was] simple, gentle, direct, unaffected . . . a magnificent human being . . . and one of the most compassionate, sensitive, gentle people I have ever known of either sex."
> —Col. (later General) Charles "Buck" Lanham

Buck Lanham observed Hemingway in northern France after D-Day and later in the battle for Hurtgen Forest in the east. Lanham believed that Hemingway considered his World War II time in the liberation of France the happiest time in his life, and he considered the writer courageous and humorous. This evaluation was altered later when Hemingway was in the grip of the alcohol jinnee.

In *True at First Light*, Hemingway says, "When you stop doing things for fun, you might as well be dead." In contrast, Norman Mailer, in his book, *On God*, said, "If you want to be a serious novelist . . . you don't have a lot of fun. You have to give up the idea of fun." (A copy of Mailer's best seller, *The Naked and the Dead*, is on the bookshelves in Hemingway's library at Finca Vigia.)

Fun was a solid plank in Hemingway's never-delineated code of values and behaviors. He was the center of ever-shifting, ever-expanding bands of admirers, from his days in northern Michigan to his pals in Paris, Key West, Sun Valley, and Cuba. They were merrymen and merrywomen, all creators and purveyors of fun in the game of life. Later, he was amazed at his personal impact on others. His realization of this led to his determination, usually, to keep it under control so that his true nature would remain intact.

To Earl Wilson, *New York Post* columnist, at the Floridita in Cuba, after signing autographs, Hemingway remarked, "What we don't want ever to do is get swellheaded."

Then there are the others.

Literally thousands who have studied Ernest Hemingway have tried to put themselves into his skin and brain. Many of them tried to extrapolate a piece of him into a whole. They have examined his every move and alleged motivations. They have attempted to "get him into them," a paraphrased quote of Henry David Thoreau made a long time ago. But no one has ever encompassed him.

Many acknowledged his popularity, his contribution to our literature, his genius, before turning on the frying pan. They psychoanalyze him in individual limited or professional ways. He has been accused of self-deception, megalomania, and being a ravager of fellow writers and friends, a liar, an exploiter of women. And that's only a few of the epithets.

In a scientific paper, psychiatrist Irvin Yalom and his wife, Marilyn, a literary scholar, concluded that Hemingway was trying to live up to an "idealized image" of himself and couldn't match his superhuman expectations of himself (Scott Donaldson, *Hemingway vs. Fitzgerald*). This idea has gained traction in academe and, in my opinion, is a complete misdiagnosis and a case of "pushing the Freud." Hemingway wasn't trying to "live up" to anything. He was what he was, extremely beyond the norm, and, perhaps, even the abnorms of the profile of the typical man.

Dr. Don Goodwin, in *Alcohol and the Writer*, suggested that the Mayo Clinic diagnosed Hemingway as a manic-depressive in 1961 (Donaldson, *Hemingway vs. Fitzgerald*). Manic-depression causes extreme shifts in mood, energy, and functioning. It's characterized by episodes of mania and depression. This is not a description of his behavior. What's more, none of the letters written by doctors at the Mayo Clinic, printed within these pages, referred once to manic-depression.

Some have posited the theory that Hemingway was schizophrenic, including his pal during the last decade of his life, A. E. Hotchner. Schizophrenia is characterized by delusions, hallucinations, and bizarre and disorganized speech and behavior. It could be argued that he was delusionary at times during the last two years of his life. Other than that, not once in his life did he display any of these characteristics.

It is true that alcohol helped bring him down. He never quit but was forced to reduce his intake during medical treatment and because of the medications he was taking in the last year of his life.

Dr. Goodwin put forth an eye-popping list of writers who were alcoholics. Here's a sample: James Agee, Truman Capote, Raymond Chandler, John Cheever, Stephen Crane, Theodore Dreiser, Jack Kerouac, Sinclair Lewis, Jack London, Edwin Arlington Robinson, William Saroyan, Edna St. Vincent

Millay, and John Steinbeck. Hemingway, it appears, was in good company. The quantities and strength of the alcohol, though, were clearly above normal and, we could argue, surpassed the intakes of the others.

Ah yes, the suicide. And the myriad complexities and questions that final act spawned.

Many are convinced that he was doomed to kill himself because others in his family did so, specifically his father first, then a sister, a brother, and a granddaughter after Hemingway's death. In my opinion, this is facile pattern seeking and gene manipulation hocus-pocus. Walter Houk (see chapter 1), a friend of Ernest Hemingway in the mid-'50s in Cuba, wrote me once his take on Hemingway's death:

I am always surprised when people demand THE cause of his death. It seems to me that eight to ten hours of drinking followed by two Seconals nightly for upwards of a decade would have some effect. So would the drinking itself. So would have such organic problems as hepatitis and seven concussions in three years, more than you should give the average writer except perhaps Mr. Andre Gide. And the aftermath of two plane crashes. Or just the effects of age past 60 or so when memory and vocabulary and other powers decline. With all that, who needs shock treatments?

Hemingway encountered enough afflictions and accidents to bring down any ordinary human. But life finally leveled him, and he ended it with two blasts of a shotgun. "Fraid o' nothing" had come full circle. Three things did it in my opinion. One was alcohol, which even he couldn't conquer in the end, in conjunction with the variety of medications he was on (see chapter 7). The second, was the shock treatments administered by Dr. Howard Rome at the Mayo Clinic, which damaged his memory, his talent, and, very quickly, his desire to live. Plus, it became obvious to him that life was no longer fun.

Also there is evidence, unsubstantiated, that he had liver cancer. He thought he did. So did Tillie Arnold and A. E. Hotchner.

Was it possible that he didn't comprehend the legend he was creating about himself, that he was unique in his impact on civilization? If he suspected it, in my opinion, he generally ignored it. He was too busy living life to examine his posterity.

There are other universal symbols such as Claude Monet and numerous artists about whom industries and literary societies have sprung, but none with the universal appeal of Hemingway. If he would have known that his persona—greatly abetted by his suicide—would have created this, perhaps he would not have killed himself. Those concluding shots, although he was not mentally right at the time, triggered what seem to be eternal interest and puzzlement, which often overshadows his legacy to literature. The suicide was the last thing expected by anyone with the exceptions of A. E. Hotchner and Tillie Arnold and, perhaps, Mary Hemingway and a few other close friends in Sun Valley.

Dr. Rome's comment to Mary in his letter of November 1, 1961, some four months after Hemingway's death, is pertinent here, further complicating the inquiry: "This kind of violent end for a man who we knew to possess the essence of gentleness is an unacceptable paradox." Indeed.

Finally, I don't believe that we can judge Hemingway with the usual standards. He lived in a realm of his own. Archibald MacLeish once said he was "God's spy on earth." My opinion is that his personality, his genius, his relationships with the high and low of us, his hard-earned knowledge and experience that gave him an uncommon judgment of what was right and wrong—all of this allowed him to create a literature for the ages.

It's axiomatic that creative people must be ego driven and ride a sliding scale of emotions every day. All those who take liberties in their *pronunciamentos* of how Ernest Hemingway thought and did what he did, those who knew him and those who didn't, are often off-base, including me.

The truth is that there is only one truth, and the only one who can speak it and explain it can't.

Inside this Book

This book is by no means a comprehensive biography of Ernest Hemingway. That has been done by many others. My intent is to provide a modicum of further enlightenment about a very complex man from those who knew him to some degree or at some level. The progenitor for this kind of biography of Hemingway was Denis Brian's *The True Gen*. Brian's book was the full dinner; mine is a "small plate."

Here are eight chapters of comments and remembrances from people who knew Ernest Hemingway, plus a final chapter with five capsule entries, including the story of the discovery of Hemingway's *Toronto Star* typewriter. In these pages are documents and photos never before published.

First, I must confess that I didn't interview everyone featured in this book. I "knew" Mary Hemingway through correspondence and Capt. Reece Dampf only through a relative of his who was a friend of mine. Of those interviewed, two survive, Walter Houk, now in his early eighties, and Patrick Hemingway, who is two years younger.

George Plimpton is not here although I was "with" him in Key West in 1985 and some time later, shortly before his death, as he took a table on the terrace of Le Dome in Paris. Also not here is Donna Kimbell, a younger sister of Tillie Arnold, who knew Hemingway in the late 1940s in Sun Valley when she and Tillie ran the Sun Valley Lodge camera shop.

Did I ever meet Hemingway? No, but I was so close. He and his bota-bagging gang of revelers enhanced the ambiance of the Pamplona Festival of San Fermin in 1959. I was there just one year later.

I hope these vignettes advance your knowledge of Hemingway.

And of course one day, perhaps people who know me will tell those they know that they knew someone who met 10 people who knew Ernest Hemingway.

CHAPTER ONE

NITA AND WALTER HOUK

In Papa's Mob

It was cigar box in size and wrapped in brown paper. The package and the box inside gave no clue of the contents. When I opened it, I saw tissue paper and beneath it, cotton wrapped around a small container. Inside, nestled on more cotton, was what appeared to be a tiny seashell about the size of a lump of sugar.

In her accompanying note, Nita said the fossilized shell had been picked up on an isolated beach on the Cuban north coast by Ernest Hemingway and then given to her with the exhortation, "Everybody needs a good luck piece." Nita had kept her precious treasure secure in her jewelry box for 38 years, and now she had decided that this Papastone should belong to me.

I had met Nita less than four years prior. It was late Saturday afternoon of November 17, 1984, when Nita answered my knock at the door of her home in Woodland Hills, California, her dog, Toro, at her side. I quickly learned that she was hooked up to portable and stationary tanks that fed oxygen through a tube to her nose. She had a rare lung disease in addition to diabetes. She and her husband, Walter, ushered me into the living room where she sat me on the couch with her. In between us were two stacks of memorabilia. Walter sat in a leisure chair opposite us. I was nervous because they were the first people I had met who were intimately connected with Hemingway and were willing to share their experiences with me.

I could perceive that Walter viewed me with caution, and of course, I couldn't blame him. All those who had known the great writer had been approached over the years by all sorts, from serious and not-so-serious biographers to booksellers and charlatans.

The Papastone, a lucky piece given to Nita Jensen Houk by Hemingway

Nita was more trusting, and we spent about two hours discussing Hemingway with Walter interjecting from time to time.

Nita's first sentence to me was "You won't publish this, will you?" I replied, "No, I know the code." Uncodified and unpublished, the Hemingway rules for living can be found in his writings, and one of them was loyalty and trust in your friends. But I wanted to remember our conversation; so I turned on my memory machine and, the next day, wrote down everything I could recall. The result, edited somewhat, follows later.

By the end of my visit, a kind of circumspect rapport had developed between the three of us. This engendered a long correspondence, not altogether surprising, as the focus of it was someone we mutually admired.

Nita and Walter in Cuba

The facts and observations in this section have been distilled from an erudite, fascinating, and as-yet unpublished book by Walter Houk with the title *Havana and Hemingway: A Mid-Century Memoir*. In published biographies of the writer, there is little written about his years in Cuba, and much of these are misleading. Walter, accurate almost to a fault, brings forth much of the truth about Hemingway during four years at midcentury, 1949 to '52, arguably Hemingway's peak of productivity in the Cuba years: *Across the River and Into the Trees*, *Old Man and the Sea*, and much of the writing for what later became *The Garden of Eden* and *Islands in the Stream*, both published posthumously.

Walter graduated from the U.S. Naval Academy in 1947 and joined the U.S. Foreign Service. His first assignment was in Guayaquil, Ecuador, as the youngest American vice-consul ever appointed. After two years, he was grateful to be assigned to Havana and arrived there by DC-6 on December 2, 1949. The embassy then was headquartered in the Horter Building, facing the Plaza de Armas and a block away from the Ambos Mundos Hotel, a Hemingway hangout in the 1930s. A block away in the other direction was the harbor of Havana and Club Nautico, where Hemingway for some time docked his fishing boat, *Pilar*. Walter's job as third secretary was to report on all facets of Cuban agriculture and encourage the Cubans to diversify from their one-crop sugar economy. Just five months before he left Cuba in September 1952 for another assignment, he was appointed to the political section.

Juanita Jensen was already ensconced behind her desk as an embassy secretary when Walter reported for duty. Nita was a civilian in army intelligence. She had been assigned to Havana from a stint in Washington DC following other tours in Panama, Guatemala, and Madrid. In Madrid, she became enamored with bullfights and Hemingway's book *Death in the Afternoon*. She was barely aboard in 1947 when Hemingway walked in on June 13 to pick up a Bronze Star he had been awarded for meritorious service in Europe in 1944. He was wearing a guayabera, or sports shirt, and loafers with no socks—in my personal view, absolutely the proper attire in warm-weather Cuba.

It wasn't until two years later when the Hemingways returned from Europe in May 1949, and he had an immediate need for secretarial help with a mountain of correspondence. He called a friend at the embassy for help, and Nita got the call. She started working on May 28. When she arrived at the Finca and entered the living room, Mary was less than welcoming, although later she became a good friend. Hemingway and Nita walked to the Little House, a detached two-story guest quarters, for Nita's first dictation duties with the man who had so impressed her. Nita remarked to me that he "was very polite . . . he seemed nice, even soft, not at all as rough as I expected . . . Not once did he say anything like a four-letter word."

After a day of work, they returned to the main house for drinks and conversation. The connection with Hemingway was made, and Nita's positive feeling was reinforced the next day when Hemingway asked her to fill in as his secretary whenever he needed her. She knew that she could do so on weekends, holidays, and after work. The bargain was sealed, although her fee was not determined until later.

Thus began a more or less regular routine of taking dictation at the Finca and then transcribing the letters and other correspondence onto stationery for mailing or filing. This was a heady experience for her, as she typed and mailed letters to Hemingway's family, to his military friends, to taxidermists, to Scribners Bookstore and other bookstores, to newspaper columnists and editors, his publishers—with the most imaginative and liveliest to Charles Scribner—to luminaries of literature such as John Dos Passos and Malcolm Cowley, and to his agent A. E. Hotchner. She also typed the manuscript for *Across the River and Into the Trees* from Hemingway's handwritten original.

After a few months, Nita convinced the writer to rent an easier-to-use Royal Standard typewriter for her, and in August 1949, he bought a wire recorder, which he called "my talk machine." He used it from then on for most correspondences.

Nita Houk "herds" cats at the Hemingways' Finca Vigia in Cuba

Over the months ahead, Nita became a part of the family, even to the point of allowing the house cats to eat off her plate. It didn't bother Hemingway or Mary to share food with their "cotsies."

Hemingway lived in Cuba for 21 years; Walter calculated that during this time, he and, later, Mary, took 16 trips of three months to more than a year, totaling seven years away from Cuba. When the Hemingways visited France and Italy from November 1949 to April 1950, Nita became the designated house sitter. She had to make payroll, feed the cats, and oversee the staff's maintenance of the gardens and swimming pool. During those months, she also had to endure a monumental display of boorishness from visitor Gianfranco Ivancich, the brother of Adriana, who was the ostensible model for the heroine Renata of Hemingway's new novel.

Nearly a year later in October 1950, Nita and Walter finally got connected at a cocktail party by an embassy friend. They quickly found mutual interests and affection, and on November 15, Nita asked Walter to drive her out to the Finca. Walter, ever the objective observer, wrote in his journal that it was "an easy-going house," but what brought a sense of awe and contemplation to him was the master bedroom, where Hemingway wrote and the Royal portable typewriter sat. It suddenly occurred to Walter that this "was where all *those* words came from."

A month later on December 14, Walter met the writer at the Finca. Walter never forgot their introduction. Hemingway gave him a firm handshake and said, "Hello, my name's Hemingway." Walter thought that he did not need to be told that, but Hemingway's demeanor was clearly unaffected. Walter described in detail in his journal his gradual introduction into the Finca community, including a detailed description of Hemingway's personal being and bearing. "He listened when you spoke and looked you in the eye knowingly," Walter wrote.

Shortly, it became natural to call Hemingway Papa, although the writer didn't ask Walter to. And it didn't take long for Walter to note that Hemingway owned a personal magnetism that encompassed those who "shared special or even privileged insight and sentiments." Walter wrote, "Papa had the curious ability to let you know you were accepted . . . without having to say so. Somehow you then became one of those who returned the feeling with an unspoken loyalty." Walter called it being "absorbed into Papa's mob."

Nita and Walter were invited often to dine with Mary and Ernest, and they agreed that Mary was an excellent cook. At dinner, Walter noted, "They drank wine, not labels."

Hemingway imbibed anything in often large quantities, and even then he would seldom show signs of drunkenness. One of his favorites was whiskey. He told Walter that the doctor had advised him to consume only one drink a day, so he drank a tall glassful, adding a small amount of water or ice cube as the day progressed.

Nita and Walter were very impressed by Hemingway's ability to tell a story. Wrote Walter, "Ernest was a gifted raconteur, fond of anecdotes, some supposedly from his past, all told so skillfully I suspected even then that they blended fact and the storyteller's art. You could not always tell when he was joshing."

Hemingway's daily attire was sports shirt or guayabera, shorts, and sandals, and maybe underwear, and he seldom altered this look. When Patrick, his middle son, was to marry in Baltimore, he refused to attend because the

Wedding reception at the Finca for newlyweds Nita and Walter

bride-to-be's mother demanded that he wear a suit. "Nobody's going to tell me what to wear," he said.

It didn't take long for Nita and Walter to realize that they were meant to be permanent partners, and on March 16, 1952, they became engaged and set the wedding date for April 30. Hemingway offered the Finca for the reception, and the couple was thrilled to accept.

The civil ceremony took place at the law offices of Lazo y Cubas in Havana, and Hemingway happily agreed to give the bride away as proxy for Nita's brother, who was in the navy and stationed far away. Hemingway, at Mary's urging, forsook his standard wear and appeared in a pin-striped suit and tie from much earlier years—and socks. He left for the Finca immediately after the ceremony, and by the time the newlyweds arrived there, he had already changed to a guayabera, white pants, and, of course, no socks.

According to Nita, "The reception was absolutely wonderful, the food unbelievable."

Don Andres, one of Hemingway's mob, contributed to the festivities by shooting off a small brass saluting cannon from the front entry—one of two situated just inside the door—and, later, skyrockets from the west terrace. Walter wrote, "The champagne flowed like the fountains of Versailles." Later, the cake was cut with Hemingway's German SS knife, and then in a "shower of rice," the couple departed for a resort at Varadero Beach outside of Havana.

All in all, Walter's journal from those days showed five fishing expeditions on the *Pilar*, Hemingway's cruiser, and 15 visits to the Finca from November 1950 to August 1952. The dates were the following:

* 1950—November 15 and December 14
* 1951—January 4; April 1; July 4, 9, 17, and 21 (first *Pilar* trip, Hemingway's 52d birthday), August 29 (*Pilar* again), October 13
* 1952—March 31, April 13 and 30, June 28, and August 25

* The other three *Pilar* expeditions were mentioned, but not recorded in Walter's journal.

It was following the July 21 birthday cruise that Walter and Hemingway visited the Floridita, Hemingway's nickname for his hangout, the bar-restaurant La Florida. It was the forerunner of today's "El Floridita," the name given by a Castro-government entity that tore down the original in the early 1990s, rebuilt a gentrified version that apparently includes the original bar,

The *Pilar* on display at the Finca

and gave the replacement its current name. Today, it is nearly a shrine to the writer, with a full-size statue of him at the corner of the bar where he usually drank. What he drank became known as the Papa Doble. Hemingway's version of the daiquiri, unlike all the abortions of it that have been claimed, was simply a double frozen daiquiri made of light rum and lime juice with crushed ice. Sugar, a usual ingredient of the recipe, was eliminated by Hemingway.

Hemingway had been working hard on completing *The Old Man and the Sea* in the winter and spring of 1952. Walter received word of his new assignment to Japan that summer, and on August 25, the couple made their last visit to the Finca. Scribner's had given Hemingway 10 copies of *Old Man*, and Hemingway inscribed one and gave it to the Houks as a farewell gift. The inscription read, "Good luck in Japan or wherever, with all affection." On September 1, *Old Man* was published in *Life* magazine; and the next day, Nita and Walter left for Japan. They never saw the Hemingways again, although there was written communication from time to time and Nita talked to Mary by phone after Hemingway died.

Walter's impressions of the great writer were truly intriguing: "Now it is hard to set down any concrete or simple impression of this man. He projects simplicity, but a simplicity born of an amazing complexity of thought. He is very human and not at all affected . . . There is a great sensitivity crowded in his big frame. He operates with subtlety and acute observation, never missing a trick. It is almost frightening."

In early 1954, the Hemingways were involved in two lightplane crashes in Africa, one right after the other. About the second one, Walter later wrote, "This time, Papa's head injuries were so severe they most likely marked the beginning of the drastic physical and mental decline he suffered in the last seven years of his life. Pouring gin into an open head wound may not have been the best therapy, either."

The Nuffer-Houk Correspondence

After my visit to Nita and Walter's home in November 1984, a correspondence ensued between us. Through emails and letters, we nurtured a pleasant acquaintanceship into a solid friendship and then beyond that to one of mutual trust and affection. How lucky that was for me, because Walter had become much more than a second secretary of embassy in the U.S. Foreign Service during his career. After a short stint in Japan, Walter parlayed his talents into a life as a journalist and an editor for *Sunset*, one of the U.S. West's most prestigious magazines. He followed two decades there with a follow-on career as a travel writer, during which he continued to sharpen his knowledge and memories of Hemingway. He became a finely tuned observer of the Hemingway scene. This, plus his prodigious memory, gave me a once-in-a-lifetime opportunity to discover the real man behind the legend of Ernest Hemingway.

Walter and I communicated regularly for the next ten years when I was still active in the Hemingway Society biennial conferences and other meetings in between. Meetings were held in Paris and some sites across the States, including Key West, Upper Michigan, Boston, and Sun Valley, Idaho. I reported on each of these to the Houks and sent them news I had picked up on other explorations.

During this time, death intervened twice. As Walter and I prepared for a much-anticipated and difficult-to-arrange visit to Cuba in 1988, two days before departure, a tragic confluence of genes born into the offspring of my oldest son and his wife brought the quick death of the baby. Our trip was cancelled. Following the graveside ceremony, I wrote to Walter noting my suspicions that often the best-laid plans once interrupted never get implemented. I hoped that wouldn't be true in our case, but it was. Life had its priorities.

That year, Walter began outlining and writing his book about Hemingway and Cuba. A major component was to be oral-history interviews that he had done with Nita. He asked me to review the manuscript chapters as they were completed, which I was pleased to do, never thinking I had much to offer, but Walter apparently thought so. Then the second intervention. On Christmas Eve of 1991, after 39 years of marriage, Nita's time expired, and she passed away. I read Walter's notification with a sigh of sadness. I wrote in my note to him, "There is no question that she, as well as you, are of the Hemingway family. As you know, I can think of no better family than that." I told Walter that I was holding the Hemingway "lucky shell," or Papastone, in my hand and was rubbing it in gratitude for Nita's generosity of spirit. I also wished her Godspeed.

In August 1993, a letter from Walter arrived with a slightly yellowed calling card inside the envelope. I was incredulous. It had a handwritten note on it signed by Ernest Hemingway. I never expected to own anything so meaningful. In my note of gratitude to Walter, I told him that I was planning my own mini museum for it. I had it framed along with a photo Walter had taken of Hemingway on the *Pilar* on his 52d birthday. The right place for it was on the cabinet between our kitchen and dining room, and it is still there today.

Hemingway's signature and message on a business card,
Christmas 1949

By 1994, Walter had 70,000 words in manuscript form, and both of us began what turned out to be an unrewarding effort to find a publisher. As noted earlier, it remained unpublished.

In 2005, yet another surprise awaited me in a large package that arrived at our door. It was a three-ring binder, and on the cover was the title *The Nuffer-Houk Correspondence, 1984-2005.* Beneath that was a 1992 photo of Walter and me and *Two Decades of Letters, Reports, and Interviews Exchanged by Hemingway Observers David Nuffer and Walter Houk.* To say that I was flabbergasted would be a mild response. Me? My papers? All I had done over the years was attend conferences, visit places of Hemingway influence, and report on them to a few friends, especially Walter, all out of passionate interest, not academic curiosity. Then I read Walter's introduction.

He referred to the 130 letters and other documents, much of which emanated from me. He talked of my interviews with people who had known Hemingway and which now form the bulk of this book. His last paragraph reads like this:

"Looking at them and reading their relatively measured language now, I believe they preserve some of the flavor and context of their era, an important element often left out of latter day judgments about the past. Their timeliness and their occasional nuggets of insight, information, and even knowledge may turn out to be valuable contributions to the record."

Walter thought that this record could someday wind up in a research library at some university. I am still incredulous, especially since I consider him to be a brilliant observer and analyst.

Walter divided the letters and papers into 12 sections. The titles alone explain much of what lies in these pages:

Part 1, 1959-1961. Hemingway at the Mayo Clinic

Part 2, 1984-1993. Acquaintance with Juanita and Walter Houk

Part 3, 1975-1985. Key West: Literary Seminar. Chat with Betty Bruce

Part 4, 1989-1995. Tillie Arnold Interviews and Correspondence

Part 5. 1989-1996. Writing and Publishing Our Books (Walter's and this one)

Part 6, 1989-1997. Conference in Sun Valley. Letters to Michael Reynolds (one of top two biographers of Hemingway)

Part 7, 1988-1989. The Ill-Fated Nuffer-Houk Havana Trip

Part 8, 1990. Hemingway Conference in Boston. Other Related Matters

Part 9, 1991. Hemingway Conference in Petoskey

Part 10, 1994. Hemingway-Fitzgerald Conference in Paris. 1953
letter to Bernard Berenson

Part 11, 1994-1995. Jose Garate. The Chiki Jai (Tijuana, Baja
California) Celebration

Part 12, 1995. A Chat with Patrick and Carol Hemingway

These papers, as organized by Walter, have, in turn, helped me organize
my material as I write this book. Highlights from these sections appear
herein.

Over the years, the Houks proved themselves masters of surprise and
generosity. Their bestowal of precious personal items to me was beyond my
understanding, but not my appreciation. I felt then, and still now, blessed.
I'm pleased to say that correspondence between me and Walter continues to
this day.

Notes from Our First Meeting

The following notes went back to my introduction to Walter and Nita
on that November evening in 1984 and the full engagement of my memory
machine that next day.

The first anecdote concerned the time Hemingway said, "Daughter, you
should bleach your hair." Mary had done it, and both she and Ernest thought
a bleach would enhance Nita's attractiveness. They knew a cosmetologist, and
one day, Mary walked into Nita's office and said, "It's time. C'mon." Both
she and Ernest watched the entire process. At one point, Ernest "reassured"
Nita by saying, "Daughter, don't worry if it comes out purple."

When Nita and Walter's wedding approached, the ambassador's wife
called a card party on the same afternoon as the wedding because she had
had some problem with one of Nita's sisters some years before, when they all
lived in the Canal Zone—something she'd never gotten over. This cut down
the number of people who attended the reception at the Finca. The pettiness
of the ambassador's wife was one of the reasons that caused Walter to get out
of foreign affairs and into writing.

Nita and Walter were guests of Hemingway on several fishing expeditions
on the *Pilar*, and although Nita claimed not to be strong enough for fishing,
she caught a dolphin or dorado once. Said Nita, "Papa was gentle, loving,
humorous unless he was drinking too early. Then he got morose."

The Hemingways tried to interest her in shooting, but after one shot,
they stopped insisting.

Nita and Walter both drank with Ernest at the Floridita, "the Cradle of the Daiquiri." Nita showed me a photo folder, and on the cover was a picture of a Spanish conquistador raising his cup in a toast, with Florida Indians behind him. Under the picture, it said, "Ponce de Leon finds the Fountain of Youth at La Florida," the bar's name in Hemingway's time. Inside was a picture of Nita and Mary.

Nita had been with the U.S. government in several places, including Spain, where she saw a mano a mano between Dominguin and Manolete, who was later gored and killed in the ring. She was enamored with bullfights and Hemingway's book, *Death in the Afternoon*.

She called Ernest a "professional man," loyal to a fault, heavily critical of what he perceived to be phonies or jerks.

The Finca's tower had four floors. Dug into the hillside below the house, the lowest level held a carpentry shop. The next level up, entered from the west terrace, was reserved for 30 to 40 resident cats and had a concrete floor that was hosed down periodically. The next floor stored luggage and other things, and the top floor was a study where Hemingway could write. From there, an outside spiral staircase led to a rooftop sunbathing deck with a low parapet. Built in 1947-48, the tower suggested the Finca's namesake, a lookout or *vigia*, but the name actually derived from an army lookout site years earlier.

Hemingway offered Nita the typescript of *Across the River*. He told her it would probably be valuable some day. Mary was standing nearby. Nita thought about Papa's kids and said, "No, it best belongs to the family."

Nita did not type *Old Man and the Sea*.

Hemingway called his new wire recorder the "Voice of Doom."

Hemingway kept names and addresses and phone numbers scribbled on the wall of the pantry, which led into the kitchen.

In his bedroom, he had stacks of mail lying on his bed, all carefully organized, and he knew what was in every pile.

Mary was tiny but tough and stood up to Ernest when she had to. One time he brought out a hooker from Havana (he said one of his drinking pals did it), and she tried on one of Mary's best dresses. This incensed Mary, and Papa became very contrite.

People would drop in all the time, and it was exasperating. Hemingway was hospitable but was sorely hurt when a favorite longtime possession, a sterling silver bottle opener, disappeared from a table by the pool.

The cats were led by Willie, or "Wiwi," as one of the servants called him. Mary would stack up a plate with ground round, and Willie would have first crack, soon to be followed by the horde of others.

Once at a party at the Club Nautico, Ernest gave Nita a big bear hug. "He would surround you with his arms. He seemed so big. It seemed like I came up to his waist."

At the same party, slightly inebriated, he danced on his toes to the hilarity of the crowd.

When the Hemingways traveled to Europe in 1949, Nita was given the assignment of living at the Finca and watching over it. The brother of Adriana Ivancich, model for Renata in *Across the River*, decided to bring his pals there for a party. Nita had little patience with Gianfranco and company since they arrived at 11:00 p.m. and raised hell, throwing food around and generally making a mess. It was a miracle that the four-by-five-foot Miro painting, *The Farm*, wasn't damaged. Nita wrote a letter about the incident to Ernest. He penciled his reply in bed at the Gritti Palace Hotel in Venice, in handwriting—slanting downward, as usual. He chided her saying that Gianfranco "was a friend. After all he was in the war," and this apparently meant everything to Hemingway.

Mary wasn't fond of Gianfranco either, but later said that he had come through in a crisis when she really needed him.

Both Nita and Mary thought Adriana was a "bitch" and that her mother was weird and crazy.

At this point in 1984, Mary was still alive and living in a penthouse in New York City. The last time Nita called her had been about a year earlier. They chatted awhile, then the nurse came on the line, and Nita asked how things were going. The nurse replied, "As well as we can expect under the circumstances."

Nita tried to call Mary the day after Ernest killed himself, but his sister, Sunny, said, "It would be a real kindness if you wouldn't talk to her."

Nita often thought of asking Mary what she really felt about the suicide because Papa had persuaded Mary to marry him by telling her, "We can grow old together."

Neither Nita nor Walter thought that Hemingway ever turned on old friends. If he did, they conjectured, he must have had a good reason.

Nita didn't know much about the sons—Jack, Patrick, and Gregory—but she said that Hemingway would "bust his buttons" over how successful Jack's daughters, Margoux and Mariel, had been. This was before they both took downward paths in their lives.

The Houks said that Hemingway once told Nita, "Anything is okay as long as it doesn't hurt someone else."

Nita and Walter several times accompanied the Hemingways on the *Pilar* to a place called Puerto Escondido. They would anchor there and swim to the beach. Papa would wear a cowboy hat to protect his face from the sun. He had a skin condition that would arise when his face was exposed to the sun.

Nita knew Betty and Toby Bruce, and her eyes lit up when I mentioned that I had met and talked with Betty on a previous trip to Key West.

The Houks owned signed first editions of *Across the River and Into the Trees*, *Death in the Afternoon*, and *The Old Man and the Sea*. Hemingway also signed the Hemingway's wedding present to Nita and Walter, *The Joy of Cooking*.

Nita still owned the actual shorthand pads she used and some transcriptions. She had several letters not included in Carlos Baker's *Selected Letters*.

Hemingway had Nita learn how to sign his name. She did so, but added a tiny fillip to the *y* so that she couldn't be accused of forgery. Hemingway also asked her to sign checks, but she demurred. Mary eventually asked Nita to learn how to sign her name too, but Nita never got around to it.

Cuba by Proxy

Through an uncanny confluence of coincidences, I was lucky in late 2004 to have an opportunity to visit Cuba—the only home of Ernest Hemingway that I had not experienced in my travels. The impetus was a "cultural and religious exchange" promoted by a Sacramento lobbyist and I was given access to it right out of the blue. That and an unexpected check from my company for earlier consultation services that covered the cost of the trip almost to the penny. Plus, the encouragement of my wife. The timing was perfect; I must have been rubbing my Papastone. So from December 11 to 14, I was in Cuba where Hemingway had lived the longest in his lifetime.

Walter and I had planned this trip 16 years earlier, but sadly, he felt he was not in sufficient physical trim to make it this time. So I became his proxy and vowed to make it as real for him as I could with photos and description. Graciously, Walter put together a Havana tour for me of "Hemingway haunts from 50 years ago." As expected, Walter's tour was exact in all details. He even placed the symbol *PH* by sites that meant "possible but by no means mandatory photo subject." I took pictures of most of these anyway.

The tour included Finca Vigia; the 14-block-long Calle Obispo, with the Floridita at one end, and the Club Nautico at the other; Central Park and the Prado, the broad thoroughfare leading from downtown to the harbor entrance

Entrance to the Finca

The dining room. Hemingway sat on a chair on the left. Straight ahead is the front entrance.

The pool where rich and poor, unknown and famous, swam

Map of downtown Havana

channel; and the sites down and off the harbor waterfront boulevard known as Avenida del Puerto and a thoroughfare known as the Malecon. It also included the places where Walter lived, the Jose Marti Monument on the way to the airport, and other places. Walter never visited Cojimar, the fishing village to the east where Hemingway tied up from time to time, but I did.

So on this four-day odyssey, religion was my guise, Hemingway was my mission, and Walter was my travel companion.

I covered virtually every spot Walter listed, plus some others. It was exhilarating to tour the Finca, to take the same route into Havana as Thomas Hudson did in *Islands in the Stream* and to drink Papa Dobles at the Floridita, which, despite a rebuilding and redecoration, still resembled the bar-restaurant of the old days. I also covered the Ambos Mundos Hotel where Hemingway stayed in 1932, '33, '34, and '36 and visited many times during his 21 years in Cuba and Cojimar to the east, which served basically as the fishing village in *The Old Man and the Sea*.

Down Obispo Street in Old Havana. American Embassy, where Nita and Walter worked, was located in the Horter Building at the right.

Temple built by fishermen of Cojimar. It enshrines a bust of Hemingway. It was dedicated in 1962.

La Terraza Bar in Cojimar, a Hemingway hangout

Above La Terraza Bar: "In this place Ernest Hemingway was accustomed to drink with his compañero Gregorio Fuentes and his fisherman friends."

The Floridita was a favorite for me, and I visited it all four days I was in Cuba. On the last day, as I sat down at the bar, the bartender greeted me with a Papa Doble. A slight smile moved a corner of his mouth. I was becoming a regular.

In my perhaps biased opinion, this trip was preordained to both occur and be successful. I accomplished all of my objectives. I met the right people, hired the right cabdrivers, drank the right drinks, did the right things, paid the right homage. I did it all with Walter on my right shoulder and just maybe the man himself on my left.

Conclusion

My friendship with the Houks had many dimensions. It is real, and it is emotional. How could it not be when we shared so much together? I could never match their generosity to me. The calling card signed by the man himself, which I look at every day of my life. That large binder of Nuffer-Houk correspondence. And of course, the Papastone. In my note of gratitude

In "Hemingway's Corner" of the El Floridita bar, author with Papa Doble in hand. A bust of Hemingway and a photo of him and Fidel Castro adorn the wall.

El Floridita at corner of Montserrate and Obispo. According to Hemingway, "The greatest bar in the world."

to Nita many years ago, I wrote her that I had always believed that a few times in everyone's life, something incredible and wonderful happens, and her gift was one of those times for me. I told her I would cherish this shell, this Papastone, as if it were gold. I added, "No, that's not right. Gold is not valuable enough."

The author, his wife Mary, and Walter Houk

So where is the Papastone now? Its home is a tiny basket just big enough to hold it. It sits on my bookshelf next to my first editions of Hemingway's unmatchable works. It is still my good luck piece, and often I rub it and sometimes carry it with me. I believe it keeps us all close.

CHAPTER TWO: PART ONE

TILLIE ARNOLD HERE

". . . my good Miss Til."

It was 5:00 p.m. on June 10, 1989, when I left my room on the second floor of Sun Valley Lodge and walked to the last room on the opposite wing, room 206. This is where Hemingway stayed in his first visit to Sun Valley in 1939 and where he wrote much of *For Whom the Bell Tolls*. The room was actually a suite of three rooms (all with balconies), a living room in the middle and bedrooms on either side of the hallway, a few feet back from the doorway to the main room where early arrivals were gathering around the bar.

I looked to the left before heading for the bar, and there in what had been Martha Gellhorn's bedroom, an elderly woman and a man were conversing. In surprised recognition, I said, "Why, you're Tillie Arnold!" She answered, "Yes, I am," and took a step or two toward me. She was obviously tiring of her talking companion.

This was the second day of a three-day conference called "Hemingway in Idaho," celebrating the 50th anniversary of the author's arrival in Sun Valley, Idaho. The conference was sponsored by the Idaho Humanities Council, the Boise State University Foundation, and Hemingway Western Studies Center. Tillie was one of the participants and, as it turned out, a conference star. I wanted to talk to her sometime during my few days there, and my hopes were more than met.

When the academics realized that Tillie was in the bedroom, they began to file in respectfully and ask her questions about Hemingway. The room was stuffy, so I opened the window and sat down on the sill. As she answered the questions with patience and good humor, she sat down beside

Balcony room 206 at Sun Valley Lodge, Hemingway's first resting
place in Sun Valley in 1939. Tillie and author smiling down.

me. Trivia is the name of the game for academics, and for me too, I guess.
I asked her if she'd like a drink, and I got her a bourbon and water. It was
as if I was her protector through the grilling that took place. We formed a
kind of bond.

Then Tillie told us some stories about the relationship between Hemingway
and her husband and her. Lloyd, whose nickname was Pappy, was the chief
of photography for Sun Valley Lodge, and Tillie managed their camera shop.
They first met the writer at breakfast on September 21, 1939, and he asked
her and Pappy to join him and Marty for cocktails that evening. When they
arrived at room 206, Hemingway complained that there was no table on
which to put the drinks and hors d'oeuvres. So Pappy brought one from their
camera shop at the Challenger Inn. When it was all arranged, Hemingway
approved with "Now that is organizoots." Tillie said that he used that word
often, especially at the picnics they were constantly having at Hemingway's
urgings—spring, summer, fall, and often when snow was on the ground.

When Hemingway made a disparaging remark about Sun Valley Lodge
and suite 206, Tillie told him of some of the prestigious people who had
stayed there. He looked at Marty with raised eyebrows, "Well! We can call
this Glamour House."

In answer to a question about A. E. Hotchner, author of *Papa Hemingway*, Tillie said, "He wasn't altogether accurate."

Tillie told the professors that she knew something was wrong with Hemingway in 1958 when he had returned to Ketchum and the "the mob" was out hunting. "I was aghast," she said, "when some ducks flew over, and Mary shot one and Papa said, 'you shot my duck.' I knew then that something was not right. He never would have said that if it weren't. He always put the woman in the best spots for shooting."

Someone asked her, "Was he drunk often? Did he get blustery and loud? Did he ever approach you?" These were rather insensitive questions for this 84-year-old lady. Unfazed, she answered with a five-minute discourse about how thoroughly enjoyable Hemingway was. She said that she had never seen him drunk and never heard him swear or tell a dirty joke. She said that she had heard and read about his dark side but that she had never seen that. She looked at the questioner directly and, with her chin trembling and eyes misting, said, "When he died I felt I had lost the best friend I ever had."

The emotionally affected author on the windowsill with Tillie telling of her kinsmanship with Hemingway

That ended the question-and-answer period; and I offered to drive her to the conference dinner at Trail Creek Cabin, but the conference sponsors heard my offer and drove her there. This was still a special place for dinner, a restaurant where Gary Cooper, Ingrid Bergman, and many others dined with Hemingway. Tillie stood in the foyer, near the bar, and told us about the parties there, how the place was expanded after World War II, and where Gary Cooper had hung from the rafters by his knees.

Gary Cooper, Hemingway, and Tillie at a party

Tillie, her husband Lloyd, and Hemingway in 1958 or '59

Hemingway, Tillie, and friend Taylor Williams

Solo Tours and the Hemingway House

On Sunday morning, I hired a cab to take me south into Wood River Valley to see the places where Hemingway and his friends hunted. Tillie told me later that Hemingway fished only one time in Idaho, that he had offered to "wet a line" in the Valley's Silver Creek for Lloyd to take some photos for publicity purposes. The creek meandered through wide, flat country where they shot birds and small game. The drive through it consumed three hours, but it was worth it to capture this scene in my memory.

Wood River Valley, south of Ketchum. Hemingway's hunting country.

The word *bucolic* perfectly describes the Wood River Valley

Then, before the scheduled Hemingway House tour, I revisited the Hemingway memorial (east of Sun Valley Lodge), the haunting bronze bust of the writer set on a tall pillar of stones. With the small stream running between it and the viewing area, it was still serene and moving as it was when I had first seen it in 1972 (see chapter eight), but the scene below was changed. Where once the memorial overlooked Trail Creek and a golf course on the other side, condos had now appeared. The trees around the memorial had initials carved in nearly all of them: "G&J," "Hal and S.G.," "April 27 I love you," and "1986 Dr. A.F." This was a desecration of a beautiful memorial. What could be more reprehensible? At a later visit, I watched a young man wearing a "Harvard"-emblazoned T-shirt carve his initials into a tree while his parents looked on.

The Hemingway Memorial off Sun Valley Road, just past Sun Valley Lodge

Ernest and Mary's resting place in the Ketchum Cemetery is appropriately understated. The pine trees at the head of the flat headstones, which were four or five feet tall in '72, had grown to 30 feet. The small wooden cross put there by the American Legion had been removed. The harmony of the place with nature was now disrupted by condos to the north.

I took the last bus of conference attendees from Sun Valley Lodge to the Hemingway House. The view from the house is expansive, bringing in the river below and much of Sun Valley to the north, and the grounds are spacious. The home is more elegant than the Key West or Finca residences. The new owners, the Nature Conservancy, have rearranged some of the interior but have tried to keep it somewhat the way it was. The blond furniture was reminiscent of the '50s.

Tillie leads the tour of the Hemingway home. Here she is pointing out the foyer where Hemingway killed himself.

The front entryway of the home where Hemingway pulled the triggers

The upstairs bathroom

Tillie led a tour of the house, and before we left, we all gathered in the kitchen for another impromptu question-and-answer session with the open and honest Tillie Arnold. An academic told Tillie that a famous picture of her and Hemingway sitting in a convertible in 1939, with his arm almost around her shoulder, was being used back east to promote a relationship between them, and he asked Tillie if she had heard about it. Tillie said that of course, she hadn't. That reminded her of a story about Carlos Baker, official biographer of Hemingway, who had come to Ketchum in the '60s to interview Tillie, among others. There had been a party at Trail Creek Cabin, and Carlos was dancing with her. Carlos, the proper Princetonian, said, "You know, Tillie, Mary says Ernest was probably in love with you." Tillie replied, "Well, I suppose I was in love with Ernest too." She paused, letting that sink in, then she added, "But I never went to bed with him." I leave Baker's reaction to the reader's imagination.

Then the same academic who asked the gratuitous question in suite 206 about Hemingway approaching her said, "Well, Tillie, if you had, Carlos would never have printed it." Tillie came right back, smiling, and said, "I'm not so sure I wouldn't have."

I hung back as the group boarded the bus so that Tillie and I were the last to leave the house. In her husband's biography, *High on the Wild with Hemingway*, Hemingway was quoted as saying to Pappy about Tillie, "Fine diamonds are indestructible." I asked Tillie as we neared the bus if she thought she would ever forget about "fine diamonds." She grinned. "No, I won't." So I said, "After meeting you, it's true." She thanked me and put her arm in mine as we walked to the bus.

Rear entrance to Hemingway's last Ketchum home, the entry most used by the Hemingways and friends.

A Friendship Forms

Thus began a ten-year correspondence, frequent at first and tapering off as Tillie aged. Her last letter to me and my wife, Mary, was dated March 25, 2000. We also met from time to time: in Ketchum; in Buhl, Idaho, where she moved after leaving Hailey; in Litchfield Park, Arizona, where she wintered for several years; twice in San Diego County; and twice at the home of her sister Donna and her husband, Virgil, in La Habra Heights, once to celebrate her 95th birthday.

During this period, we talked and wrote often about the man she called Papa. And I gave her tapes and videos I had collected of Hemingway and reports of my Hemingway meetings around the country. At the same time, she and Sun Valley author Bill Smallwood were writing her own biography, to pin down for readers what Hemingway meant to her and her friends. I tried to help, but it was Bill's project of love for Tillie. The book, published in 1999 as *The Idaho Hemingway*, was not a commercial success, but it is a treasure chest of inside information.

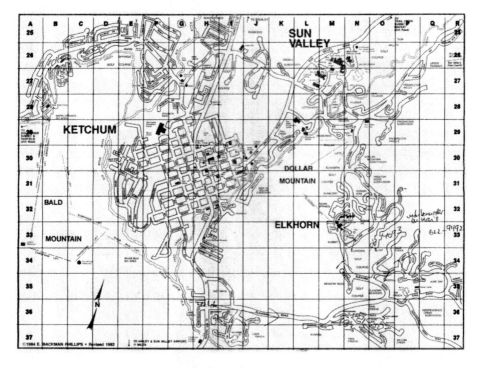

Map of Ketchum in 1993

This book revealed what Tillie knew about the man, things no one else had known. There were interviews with everyone alive then who had known Hemingway in Idaho, and most unveiled much about his personality and the way he lived. First son Jack Hemingway wrote in the foreword that Tillie's book "will rekindle a view of the human side of my father's complex character, the aspect of Hemingway all too easily brushed aside by the scholars, the critics, the sycophants, and the newcomers to his work."

Jack's father visited Ketchum and Sun Valley eight times over the years from 1939 to 1961, often for three months or more each time:

* Fall of 1939—When Ernest first met Tillie, he called her "Tillie the Toiler" after a popular comic strip of the 1920s and '30s.
* Fall of 1940—This is when he and Gary Cooper first met and a friendship began
* Fall of 1941
* Fall of 1946—He and Mary, his fourth wife, stayed at MacDonald's Cabins, now known as Ketchum Korral.
* Fall of 1947 into '48
* Fall of 1948
* Fall of 1958 to '59—They returned after a long hiatus and rented the Heiss house in Ketchum, moving to the Whitcher house when the Heisses returned.
* Fall of 1960 to July 2, 1961—They bought and moved into the Bob Topping house overlooking the Big Wood River from the west. Mary kept the house for several years after his death until she moved to New York City, off Central Park, and sold the house to the Nature Conservancy.

The Irrepressible Tillie

My wife's initial meeting with Tillie, and my second, was at her apartment in Litchfield Park, Arizona. Afterward, we spent the evening at the Wigwam Restaurant nearby. In my notes, I described the 87-year-old Tillie thus: "Beautiful full cheeks, fallen with the gravity of age, but unable to block the cuteness of her smile even now. The lines running from the corners of her mouth to her chin were deep. Her hair was white and she wore purple stone leaf earrings that spread across her earlobes. A long strand of purple stones hung from her neck. She wore a patterned dress of purple, green, and brown. Her giggle was infectious, her sense of humor pointed and pervading.

Her self-deprecating, mischievous smile was warming and fun. Later, at the Wigwam, where she downed several bourbon and waters, she even danced with much energy."

Mary, my wife, told me later that she was impressed by her elegance and style and her attire that had a designer look. "Her hair was perfectly coifed, and her nails were manicured with bright pink polish." Tillie reacted positively to Mary from the beginning, and we all became close friends over the next 13 years.

Tillie at 95

Hemingway's Mannerisms

Over the years, Tillie revealed to me her observations and nuances of Hemingway's behavior and personality. These don't appear in her book or anyplace else for that matter, at least in my research:

* "Papa had a way of talking that was different and unduplicatable. He loved to tell stories but not dirty jokes. He would laugh and shake over his stories, his shoulders jerking up and down. He would talk with his hands, but not flailing around; he would use them to emphasize points, with hands vertical or palms up"

* "He had a problem with Ls, but it wasn't a lisp. And when he spoke, he would sometimes repeat a phrase. It wasn't a stutter. It was more like an emphasis."
* "Often he would knock on wood three times, betraying his superstitious nature. He also carried around a bag of lucky pieces. He gave a piece of rhino horn to Lloyd and to Taylor Williams, the spent cartridge from the first elk he had shot. Taylor had never shot an elk."
* "He walked on the balls of his feet, as if he were on springs, and he took long strides."
* "When he was telling you something confidential or was trying to make an important point, he would lower his voice and point to his head, implying that his brain had discerned the truth. Often he would say, 'Truly, daughter, truly.'"
* "He was shy, really, he was."
* "He never was crude, at least around me."

Tillie's Insights

In the beginning, Tillie called Hemingway by his first name. But when he returned to the Valley with his three boys, she noted that they called him Papa. Tillie said it was so easy to refer to him as Papa—that both she and Lloyd did so. Oddly, she never called Lloyd by his nickname—Pappy.

Tillie's second letter to me was an eight-pager, handwritten on December 6, 1989, in Litchfield Park, where she had joined Bill Smallwood to work on the book they were compiling. He was wintering there and working on other books as well. In the letter, Tillie wrote, "I would think in my own mind that Papa would approve our efforts on the message we are trying to convey, just what he was like here. His comment would be"—and here she invoked Papa's spirit—"'Daughter, you showed me as I truly was and we had wonderful times, but you won't be able to convince the hard-core bastards that I wasn't a drunk and a fighter at the drop of a hat—sure I've done plenty of that in my life, but I wasn't bad all the time. I could be a good boy. Next time you write something, just ask for my help; you can have a bestseller.'"

Three months later on March 21, 1990, she commented on the death of her husband, Lloyd, on that day twenty years before, just ten days short of their forty-second anniversary. She wrote, "A long time, twenty years! And to be alone." And in the vein as the previous message she imagined from Hemingway, she said that one time Papa had said to her, "Wait until I'm dead.

The press will have a field day, and most of it will not be good, but you will know when it is not true and also when it is plain bullshit."

What actually happened on Hemingway's death was reams of praise and eloquent eulogies from around the world. Perhaps the best was from Archibald MacLeish, a friend in Paris, a Librarian of Congress, and Pulitzer Prize winner. Then the gravediggers began their work, proving he was right after all.

Further on, in Tillie's eight-page letter, she gave a rare and insightful thumbnail analysis of her friend. Because of its import, it follows in toto:

David, you mentioned that some academics have a theory that Ernest created himself and that he was a phony. I have felt in my own mind that Papa did a lot of things earlier in his life to call attention to himself and, of course, we know that he wrote about himself under assumed names in his stories. He knew what he was doing, and it certainly got him a lot of attention. He needed all the publicity, good or bad, that he could get when he was starting out. Then, of course, the public and the reporters added to it with a lot of stuff that was untrue. As time went on Papa forgot that he had caused a lot of it himself, especially now that he had it made. He was the best writer of fiction, comparing him to Shakespeare, etc., but the reporters he called interrupters. In *The True Gen* by Denis Brian, he was reported as being crazy and I think it was Hotch [A. E. Hotchner] that said he was insane. I can't remember just how he said it, but it would have made you feel he was a dangerous man. I say he wasn't always right on the ball but he was still smart enough to know what was going on and he was smart enough to know if he was taken away again (to the Mayo Clinic), it wouldn't be to Rochester, where he knew he could con them, but a place where he would be locked up forever and he was not one to be cooped up. He knew he wouldn't have anything more to say about his life. The only choice he had was to take his own life. I think if he had been taken to a place like Menningers in the first place he could have been helped and it is known that people who have had shock treatments can return to normal after about six months and they can remember again. But when he couldn't remember, and he said he couldn't write any more, that was the end of his will to live. I could be wrong about all of this, but I don't think so. Well enough of Dr. Tillie Arnold! Just one more thing . . . he was never a phony!

In the same vein, in one of her last letters to us on March 25, 2000, before she began to fail, she wrote, "He knew I was not a phony and he could tell me anything and it would not be repeated, and sometimes, he would say, 'It is our secret.'"

Tillie told me that Hemingway knew he had cancer of the liver and implied that a doctor at Mayo had told him. Once, when someone said that he had a cancer removed from his face, Hemingway pointed to his midriff and said he had one of those.

The Boston Hemingway Conference

The biennial Hemingway Society 1990 meeting was held in Boston in July at the John. F. Kennedy Library. The top Hemingway academics were there, plus some celebrities such as Jackie Kennedy, Norman Mailer, and Barnaby Conrad. Approximately 250 attended. Hemingway had his supporters and his detractors among the academics, and I duly reported to Tillie my observations and contempt for those who were off base. Her responses, most of them regarding Norman Mailer's keynote remarks, bear repeating here:

Mailer: "He had no routine days."

Tillie: "I think he had routine days, especially when he was writing, getting up at daylight and writing until noon and sometimes later. I think that is routine. It was routine that he did some type of exercise every day when he was able."

Mailer: "He had a prodigious competitiveness."

Tillie: "I know he did. That was excitement and I know he played to win, and when he didn't, he would be disappointed. His writing was a good example. He tried to write the best he knew how, and that was competing with all of the top writers that he knew. He knew he was good but he made a remark to us once when he was searching for a title for *For Whom the Bell Tolls*, and he read John Donne's famous prose that wound up as the preamble to the book. 'Christ, if a man could write like that!'"

Mailer: "Toward the end, Ernest had a sense of dread, that each night he would put the barrel of a shotgun in his mouth and touch the trigger, but not far enough to go off. By doing so, he rid himself of the dread for another day. Then one morning he went too far. So, Ernest did not commit suicide."

Tillie: "I have not called it a 'sense of dread.' I wasn't smart enough to think of it. But I have always maintained that he did not want to do it. I think the thought was in his head for a long time, and he couldn't rid himself of it. It was like some powerful source behind him that was stronger than he was, telling him he had to do it. He had left nearly everything behind in Cuba. He thought he was broke [not true]. He was beginning to feel like an animal being cornered and no place to go. He knew he wasn't a well man; his blood pressure was high. Well, I could go on, but anyway, he finally shot himself rather than to be shut up some place behind bars like a caged animal, when he had always been free to roam anyplace he wanted. I think he put it off as long as he could; however, if he hadn't been stopped, it would have happened earlier."

The comments at a panel the next day especially irritated Tillie. The assertion was made that Hemingway was an abusive husband, verbally and physically, that he thought of women as devouring bitches. He said that Ernest's suicide was "infantile" because he made sure that everyone had to step over his remains in the vestibule to get into the house.

Tillie said that the professor was "tetched in the head. I can believe that Papa might give someone a good tongue-lashing, but he was never physically abusive to any woman. And he should have known that the front entrance and vestibule were never used. Everyone who came to the house used the back entrance as Papa and Mary did. If anyone ever went to the front of the house, it was a stranger."

Tillie was amused by my description of the women on another panel who talked about the "feminine subversion" in *For Whom the Bell Tolls* and how women were "trivialized." She wrote, "David, you should have stood up and said, 'Was *Pilar*, one of the great women in fiction, trivialized?'" She was right; I should have. Then when I told her about other women professors talking about Hemingway's obsession with hair, something new to me, or about what academe calls "gender issues," Tillie's comment was that she would bet that those women "would have stuttered all over the place if Papa had been there and showed them some of his charm. They are the kind that would have a made a 180-degree turnaround and done handsprings for him. I say this, and I am a woman."

My Tillie Notes

Four times during the course of our friendship, I took notes during or following our meetings or discussions. They may seem disorganized, but that's only because they are. I was writing down Tillie's insights and comments about Hemingway, and they occurred randomly. Ordinary conversation isn't always logical. Here are edited versions of each.

The Wigwam, April 13, 1992

Notes from an evening with Tillie at the Wigwam Restaurant in Litchfield Park, Arizona; our first time together since the Hemingway conference in Sun Valley in 1989:

About Hadley, Hemingway's first wife, and Paul Mowrer, her second and last husband: "I met Hadley twice, once with Paul and once after Papa died. I told her that 'Ernest would have wanted to stay with you.' She shook her head, 'Nooo, it was best for him. I didn't think so at first but it was, and it was definitely best for me.'"

About Martha Gellhorn, who was yet to become the third Mrs. Hemingway: "In 1939 I told Marty to make sure she was doing the right thing in marrying Ernest."

"When Ernest, Hadley, and Bumby left Toronto in 1924, they skipped out on the rent. Hadley was afraid that they would be apprehended."

"Whenever he would walk into a room, people would stop and look."

"He once told me, 'You don't cross the line of a friendship. It's more durable that way . . . and it can't endure if you try to take it further.'"

"I never saw him drunk." Only once did he ask her to drive him home after an evening of drinking.

In an inscription to Tillie in his book *Winner Take Nothing*, he wrote, "Winner Take Nothing, me take Tillie."

In Tillie's copy of *Death in the Afternoon*, he inscribed, "Such a big book for Hemingstein to have written day and night for such a long, long time—Sun Valley, 1939."

In her copy of *In Our Time*, he penned, "Earliest book by Hemingstein. X. His mark."

"He called Somerset Maugham Somersault Moom."

After her husband, Lloyd, died, Tillie felt she made contact with him through several dreams. One time she was at a barbeque at Trail Creek Cabin, and she looked to her left and "there was Lloyd with a plate and a big steak hanging over the edges."

Buhl, July 26-30, 1993

Notes from a visit with Tillie in Buhl, Idaho:

"Once, Papa asked Patrick and Greg who I looked like. They both said, 'Our mother,' who was Papa's second wife, Pauline."

"I'd rather be a wing-shot champion than anything else," Hemingway told Tillie. Even when he was sick, she said, "He was a crack shot. He'd go down to the Big Wood River—there weren't any houses around then—and shoot traps."

Chuck and Flossie Atkinson, Hemingway friends, now buried near him, built the Christiana Motel in Ketchum in 1958 with 18 units. The motel was eventually expanded to about 38 rooms.

She and Lloyd built a home in Ketchum at the southeast corner of 6th and Walnut and lived there from 1947 to 1969.

Tillie and Lloyd Arnold lived in this modest home near downtown Ketchum for 22 years.

After Lloyd died in Phoenix on March 21, 1970, she drove to Ketchum and was seen by Mary Hemingway, who invited her to live with her in the Ketchum house and stay there when Mary went to New York City. Tillie lived there during the winter of 1970-71 through the summer of 1973. Then she flew to New York City with Mary and stayed with her for six weeks. According to Tillie, Mary developed a heavy drinking habit around 1976 after she had returned from a book convention in Germany where someone had said something very nasty to Mary. Tillie thought it concerned the keys to the gun locker downstairs the night before Hemingway killed himself. Tillie thought that this incident raised a heavy guilt in Mary. Altogether, Tillie visited Mary in New York three times. The last time, she decided that it wasn't worth the trip anymore because Mary "was so hooked on booze."

Mary begged Tillie to stay, but Tillie told her, "I can't stay here and see you destroy yourself. If you'll get help, I'll stay right with you." Tillie told her that she was losing weight from anxiety, pounds she couldn't afford to lose. "Mary never forgave me," Tillie added.

Said Tillie, "When we heard she had broken her elbow, I knew how she did it. There was a small step between rooms; and if you were drunk, you could easily misstep and fall."

According to Tillie, the only original furniture remaining in the Ketchum house is in the living room.

The base of the monument to Hemingway, just beyond Sun Valley Lodge, on the way to Trail Creek Summit, was built by Lloyd Arnold. He dug shale from soil in the area.

The famous Papa picnics were not gourmet. The group often built a fire and roasted hot dogs. Once, Tillie couldn't get a can of beans to heat up, which greatly amused Hemingway.

At home, Mary made chili—remainder sirloin tips cut in cubes by Tillie, then folded into Mary's soup. The soup was constantly going at the Hemingway house. One time, Mary threw in the remainder of a peanut butter sandwich.

Tillie related descriptions of two parties at the Hemingway house during his last months. At one time, the gang was singing songs in the kitchen while Hemingway watched sullenly from the couch in the front room. They were not having much luck with the words. Finally, Hemingway appeared in the kitchen, sang the complete words of the song, and marched off upstairs to bed. At another, a group of about 14 had gathered. Six of them, including Mary and good friend, Bud Purdy, were sitting on pillows on the floor eating off a bench because there wasn't room at the table. Hemingway turned to Tillie on his right and asked, "Where's Bud Purdy? He should be here," meaning next to him. Tillie offered, "I'll get him, Papa." He replied, "Would you do that?" Tillie told him yes and changed places with Bud.

In all her years, she heard Hemingway tell only one dirty joke: There was a price war between Checker Cab and Yellow in New York City. The drivers were scrambling for passengers. A Yellow cab driver stole away a "big-boned" woman from a Checker cab and drove off. The Checker cabbie roared up alongside the Yellow cab and hollered, "Where did you get the fat lady?" The

Yellow cabbie thought for a second and yelled back, "Why don't you take a flying kiss on the lady's ass?" Then he turned around to the backseat and said, "That's telling him, ain't it, fat lady?"

Driving home from a picnic in the late '50s, Tillie and Hemingway were in the front seat with Floyd "Duke" McMullen driving. Mary and Lloyd and Taylor Williams were drinking gin from a flask in the backseat. Hemingway was imitating an English general. Mary, a little under the weather, sneered, "Yeah, General Sonufabitch." Her husband said in his accent, "Anybody who calls me that is usually running." After the six reached the Heiss's home, where the Hemingways were staying, Mary offered the flask to her husband. He tasted it and said, "Jesus Christ, you're drinking that stuff?" and threw the flask into Trail Creek Canyon.

Tillie believed that toward the end, Hemingway's only true friends were in Ketchum. The writer had come to the area where tourists made friends with those who worked there, but as Tillie noted, it was not that way anymore.

Lloyd's last photograph, of a sheep drive on a hill above Ketchum, was framed and hung in Tillie's mobile home. And the skin of a Thompson gazelle that Hemingway shot in Africa adorned Tillie's couch. Taylor Williams brought it back from Cuba after a visit there, and when Taylor died, his son gave it to Tillie.

Telephone Call, June 11, 1995

Tillie called from Buhl and read to me what she had written the night before for the prologue of her book of reminiscence about Hemingway, to be titled *The Idaho Hemingway*. She thought it would be a good opening for the book, and I agreed, although she didn't read it all to me. It was her description of Hemingway's funeral at the Ketchum cemetery. What she read to me did not appear in the final version of the book. Paraphrased, it went like this:

We drove to the gate of the small cemetery where a guard cleared us for entering. I felt very close to Papa. He was talking to me in a low voice. "It's okay, daughter, this is the way it has to be. You're going to be swamped with people, and they will write a lot about me, things you never heard of. I told you many times that I didn't want to be a celebrity." He had told me that before, in 1939, and I'd replied that he was already a celebrity, that it was a little late to worry about it now. His voice continued, "I know your feeling for old Papa will always be the same." I could see his brown eyes twinkling and his expressive hands gesturing.

Marlene Dietrich wanted to come to the funeral, but Mary wouldn't invite her. She was jealous of Marlene. I learned later that she was jealous of me.

I asked Tillie if Hemingway liked baseball. She replied, "He sure did. When we couldn't find a good radio signal in Ketchum, we would take a lunch and go up Penny Mountain and listen to the games on his car radio."

"In 1939, Papa told me there were three reasons acceptable for committing suicide. I can't remember one of them, but number one was if you were a prisoner of war and were being tortured. The second was if you had an incurable disease. Of course, at the end, we all knew he was sick, probably with cancer of the liver. I think he knew that too. One time, after his boys had brought back some elks and they were slaughtered, Papa said, 'I think I'll check the elk livers to see if I can turn mine in for a good one.'"

The True Gen about Tillie and Hemingway

The timing of the first item was lost somewhere in my papers, but it was probably in the early forties.

"Everyone was gone, and he asked me to dinner. He drove the car, which he didn't like to do, especially at night, because of a bad eye. We ate at the Alpine. Everyone loved the Alpine food, and you could eat for almost nothing. Afterward, he drove back to the Lodge, and he invited me up to his room. I was smart enough to know that he didn't have any etchings, so I told him that was not a smart idea. So he turned his car around and drove back to the Christiana Motel where Lloyd and I were staying. He came in and looked at the books in the bookcase and, after a while, left.

"The next morning, when I opened the photo shop, he was there. He couldn't wait to tell me that a mutual acquaintance who had borrowed two of his books tried to return them at dawn. 'He was hoping to catch us together,' Papa deduced. Then he said, 'Daughter, that was the right thing you did last night. You're smarter than I am.' I told him, 'No, I was not smarter. I just had more common sense. Besides, it's first and foremost the way to destroy a most wonderful friendship.'"

I once asked Tillie, after we had become good friends, if she ever had any regrets about not going up to his room. She was adamant. "No regrets." I also asked if Lloyd was ever jealous. "No," she replied, "he knew me."

Tillie continued, "I used to pick him up when he was on his walks. He wouldn't let anyone else pick him up. And I'd drop him off wherever he wanted, but never at his home. Often we'd sit in the car in front of my house and chat. One day, he suggested we go up to the Lodge. When we got there, he offered to have a drink in the Eddie Duchin Room. I told him, 'Papa, we would be in there for 10 seconds and Mary would know.'

"Once, we were driving with son Patrick in the front seat with us. Suddenly, Patrick blurted, 'Miss Til, you have beautiful hands.' Papa and I looked at each other and smiled. He said, 'Mouse, she has useful hands.'"

In March 1961, when Lloyd and Tillie were being honored on their 33rd wedding anniversary, Hemingway called and asked if Lloyd was going to wear a tie. The writer was to live barely three months more, and he said to Tillie in a low, emotional voice, "Gee, Miss Til, I wish it were me."

"When he told me he was contemplating suicide, I told him, I don't want you to do that. You're my best friend, you're the best friend I ever had. He said that there was no other way out for him. He said that he was not going back to Rochester where 'they will lock me up.' He said that he wasn't going. I remember looking at him in the eye and telling him, 'I don't blame you, Papa.'"

He did go, though, and right after his return in late June 1961, he committed suicide.

The Hemingway table in the corner of the Christiana Restaurant in Ketchum. Ernest and Mary and friend George Brown dined here on July 1, 1961.

Tillie and Lloyd were sitting on their front porch of their home having a cup of coffee on Sunday morning when a friend came up to them and said, "Well, he done the job." He pulled the triggers at 7:30 a.m.

Mary called Tillie for help, and she drove there immediately. She went upstairs to get Mary's comb and toiletries to take her to the hospital and, coming back downstairs, saw two women cleaning up the mess in the vestibule.

"I had a very glamorous life and didn't realize it."

Dr. George Saviers, 1989

On a September afternoon in Ketchum, Tillie and Bill Smallwood, a collaborator on her book *The Idaho Hemingway*, visited Dr. George Saviers in his home. The subject turned out to be the riddle surrounding Hemingway's behavior and the way he treated people. Tillie wondered, "Was there an Idaho Hemingway and another Hemingway who was not like him?"

There was much discussion about Hemingway's drinking, even in the '30s, when he wrote *Death in the Afternoon*. They recalled that his friend, army officer Buck Lanham, described Hemingway as brave and modest in battle, but later on in Cuba, he was loud and boastful. Bill said that there would be 100% agreement in Idaho that Hemingway was a "kind, humble, generous, sensitive, playful, mischievous, loyal, polite gentleman. Yet, when you read the biographers . . . you come away thinking that he was a liar, braggart, backstabber, immodest philanderer." The two-sided man showed classic signs of alcoholism.

Tillie said that Ernest felt bad about what he had done to people, especially his old friends. He said he never would have done anything to hurt his friends if he had been sober. And the three discussants were sure that he was different in Idaho because he needed friends around him, and he wouldn't have any if he drank as much as he had been.

The consensus was that there was an Idaho Hemingway different than the one portrayed in other parts of the world.

Probably, but in this author's opinion, he behaved elsewhere much as he did in Idaho. He had friends in other places, but alcohol, especially in the quantities he imbibed, plus a damaging airplane accident in 1954 and questionable medications, clearly led to his downfall.

The Book Signing

It took a while, ten years, but Tillie and Bill Smallwood finally published her book, *The Idaho Hemingway*, in 1999. That event called for a book signing in Ketchum, and it occurred in July 23, 1999, at the ExLibris Bookstore near Sun Valley Lodge. Mary and I flew to Sun Valley for the celebration, surprising Tillie, who, momentarily forgetting our names, introduced us to her friends as "Jack and Jill."

Sitting inside the store at a round oak table were Tillie, Bill, and Jack Hemingway in shorts and a baseball cap. Jack, Hemingway's first son, was 76 years old then, and died unexpectedly in New York a few years later. On the table were the books to be signed and a bronze bust of Hemingway.

It was a joyous occasion as a constant stream of fans and admirers paused at the table to get books autographed. Tillie was 94 with a nearly permanent exterior brace to hold her back together, but you could not discern in her any discomfort or fatigue. She was one tough, lovable old gal. And she looked 20 years younger in her yellow, white, and red blouse and gold circle earrings.

Hemingway's first son, Jack, and Tillie at a book-signing event in Ketchum

Bill Smallwood and Tillie, coauthors of *The Idaho Hemingway*, at book signing with a bust of Hemingway.

We dined with Tillie and sister Donna twice during that short trip, once at a popular restaurant where Jack and his family were dining too. Then we enjoyed a meal at the Christiana Restaurant, at a table next to where Hemingway and Mary and their friend, George Brown, dined on July 1, 1961, the night before the suicide.

The Penultimate Goodbye

This farewell was poignantly described by Tillie in her book. She had told me the story earlier, so in paraphrase:

Toward the end of November 1960, amidst considerable concern about Hemingway's odd, often paranoid, and nasty behavior, Mary held a dinner party at their home as a farewell for Tillie and Lloyd who were leaving for California for three weeks of work. The whole crew of friends were there. Afterward, Lloyd went out to warm up the engine, and Tillie followed. Ernest came up to Tillie and buried her in his arms. She could feel his racing heart against her, "Oh, Miss Til, my good Miss Til." He held her hand, reluctant to let go.

When Tillie got into the car, she was crying. She said "Lloyd, he's going to die."

When they returned in December, they learned that Dr. Saviers had flown Hemingway to Rochester on November 30 and registered him in the Mayo Clinic. Thus began the tragic series of shock treatments that preceded his death seven months later.

Tillie outlived Hemingway by 46 years.

CHAPTER TWO: PART TWO

TILLIE ARNOLD THERE

A Proper Send-off

Tillie Arnold crossed the river on January 19, 2005, three months short of her century birthday. Her sister, Donna, sat by her side, holding her hand, thinking of all the work that Tillie's now-frail hands had done in their lifetime. There was no recognition from Tillie, but Donna was sure that she heard Donna tell her of her love and how good she had been to her and their four sisters and four brothers. "Like a second mother," Donna said later. "She was the oldest, 15 years older than me, and she had more common sense than anyone I had ever known. Her attitude was always positive, and she had an original sense of humor." In my opinion, those last two qualities endeared her to Hemingway.

Donna and family made the right and brilliant decision to hold the funeral and interment six months later in Ketchum on July 21, Hemingway's birthday. I sent out obituary notices to news media throughout the country. And planning began.

Five years earlier, with Tillie's agreement, I contacted the Ketchum Cemetery to find a burial plot for her there. I was surprised that she and Lloyd didn't already have plots, but Tillie told me that they did, next to Papa and Mary. When Jack Hemingway's wife, Puck, had passed, she gave the plots to Jack. Ernest must have had his hand in this when I called because the secretary-treasurer of the Cemetery Board, Wanda Glasmann, pulled strings to secure a newly available plot 399-C, immediately below and one plot to the left of those of Ernest and Mary at plots 447-A and 447-D. Considering its location, Tillie's final resting place was inexpensive at $1,200.

Tillie and Donna then decided that Lloyd's remains should join Tillie when the time came. Lloyd had died in Phoenix, Arizona, on March 21, 1970, at the age of sixty-three. He was buried in Council Bluffs, Iowa, where Tillie and Lloyd first met. For some reason, Tillie never made the final decision to disinter and cremate him and send his cremains to California. After Tillie was gone, my brother, who was a mortician, helped smooth the way with the Council Bluffs cemetery, and the task was accomplished with no problems and little cost. Donna now held the ashes of both as we prepared for July 21.

There was much to be done, and all of us, including Bill Smallwood, joined in an effort of love to make this ceremony memorable. We commissioned the Wood River Chapel in Hailey, Idaho, to handle the interment; arranged for the reception at the Sun Valley Lodge with the help of Shannon Besoyan, a publicist there; developed a program for the services or, as we called it, "The Send-off of Pappy and Tillie," using Hemingway's favored word for funeral; contracted with a still photographer and a videographer to record the event; wrote the media announcement and produced the printed program; plus a host of additional chores. Donna had invitations printed and sent them to her list of 26 friends and others at the beginning of July. I disseminated the announcement to the media shortly thereafter, and a reporter from Boise with the Associated Press picked up the story, and it ran nationwide. The coverage was enormous.

Cover of program for interment of Lloyd "Pappy" Arnold and Tillie Arnold

In Loving Remembrance

Lloyd R. (Pappy) Arnold   Tillie (Erma) Arnold
July 31,1907 - March 21, 1970   April 6, 1905 - January 19, 2005

Graveside services and Interment at
Ketchum Cemetery, 10:30 a.m., July 21, 2005
(The birth date of the Arnolds' close friend, Ernest Hemingway)

Presiding: David Nuffer
Participants: Donna Kimbell, Bill Smallwood

Pappy and Tillie..."will be here in the winter and in the spring and in the
summer and in the fall. In all the seasons there will ever be."
Ernest Hemingway
(from Gene Van Guilder's eulogy - 1939)

The interment program

The interment ceremony was blessed. The weather behaved, all the
assistants came through, and there were as many folks there as had attended
the great writer's funeral on that spot 44 years and 16 days earlier. And as
officiant, I was pretty good too. The program consisted of Bill Smallwood
and sister Donna Kimbell. Donna also had lived in Ketchum, from the end
of World War II to around 1950, and worked with Tillie in the camera shop.
She knew Hemingway and partied with him and his pals. I gave her 12
minutes to talk, and she took 30. I did my best to shorten her presentation
by looking at my watch, coughing, and moving to the podium, but we all
laughed as Donna continued to the end of what she wanted to say. As the
Idaho Mountain Express said in its story, "She charmed the gathering with
her laughter and spirit." Many of her remarks centered on Tillie's husband,
Lloyd. "You missed something if you didn't know Lloyd Arnold. They were
really a team. They both had great senses of humor." She closed by reading
a letter of condolence and remembrance from Maria Cooper, daughter of
Gary, who wrote that Tillie and Pappy were now together in "the arms of
the Sawtooths."

Interment ceremony at Ketchum Cemetery, the author presiding.
Ernest and Mary buried close by to the left.

Tillie's sister, Donna, delivers a moving eulogy

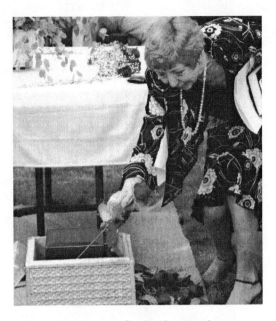

Sister Donna pays final tribute to her sister

After the eulogies, Lloyd's nephew placed his uncle's urn in a gold-painted vault, and Virgil Kimbell, Donna's husband, did the same for Tillie's. Family members and friends then placed single-stemmed red roses on the urns. And it was over.

A further description of this epiphany of sorts for me follows as part three of this chapter. My friend, Walter Houk, sent my follow-up description of the event to *North Dakota Quarterly*, a literary college journal that specializes in Hemingway, and it ran in the Winter and Spring 2006 issue.

When authors sign their books to friends and buyers, their inscriptions are usually off-the-cuff, sometimes humorous and brief because time is short for any message of depth. In our copy of *The Idaho Hemingway*, Tillie took some extra time to pen an entire page. Mary and I will forever cherish her last paragraph:

> But there is one thing I know, you would fly around the world to bring joy to my heart. You are both the light of my life.

My mark X
Tillie Arnold
7/25/99

Vol. 31-B, No. 69 • FRIDAY, JULY 22, 2005 • www.sunvalleycentral.com   One copy free

WOLF TALES
Idaho book, movie celebrated
Page 17

IDAHO MOUNTAIN

Express

AND GUIDE

CASTING CLINIC
Fishing is for everyone
Page 22

'Here in all the seasons that will ever be ...'

Tillie and Lloyd Arnold come to rest near Hemingway

By DANA DUGAN
Express Staff Writer

Express photo by David N. Seelig
Donna Kimbell places a rose on the urns of her sister Tillie Arnold and brother-in-law Lloyd Arnold at a ceremony in the Ketchum Cemetery, Thursday, July 21. The Arnolds, who were close friends of Ernest and Mary Hemingway, are now buried near them in the cemetery.

Together again after three and a half decades, Tillie and Lloyd Arnold were reunited Thursday, July 21, when their remains were interred at the Ketchum Cemetery, immediately diagonal to the graves of their dear friends Mary and Ernest Hemingway.

The day was chosen because it was Hemingway's 106th birthday. Tillie Arnold died in January of this year. Her beloved husband, Lloyd, who was known as "Pappy," died in 1970 and had been buried in his hometown of Council Bluffs, Iowa.

The burial of the Arnolds helps complete the circle of friends Hemingway made during his many years in Idaho. Near his grave are the graves of his fourth wife, Mary, as well as other members of his family, including his son Jack.

His friend Chuck Atkinson is also within the circle that surrounds Hemingway's tree-shaded burial site.

Inside the program for the "Send-Off," Hemingway was quoted from the eulogy he delivered for friend Gene Van Guilder's Ketchum funeral in 1939.

"Pappy and Tillie ... 'will be here in the winter and in the spring and in the summer and in the fall. In all the seasons there will ever be.'"

David Nuffer, a Hemingway fan and author of "A Walkable Feast," about Hemingway's days in Paris, helped Tillie Arnold's sister, Donna Kimbell, with the memorial service. He and Tillie had become friends in 1989 and remained so until her death. During Kimbell's story-filled eulogy for her older sister and brother-in-law, Nuffer kept tabs on how long she was talking, much to her amusement.

Bill Smallwood, a Ketchum resident and co-author of Tillie's book, "Hemingway in Idaho," said, "Hemingway's friends meant everything to him. He was a little insecure, and writing is a lonely job. You need to be with people who stimulate you. He needed intelligent people and he cherished *See FRIENDS, Page 12*

Local coverage of the event

Papa's pals

AP photo

This 1958 photo provided by the Regional History Department of the Ketchum Community Library shows from left: Lloyd Arnold, Ernest Hemingway, Tillie Arnold and Mary Hemingway, after a day of hunting near Sun Valley. Part of Hemingway's circle of Idaho friends, the Arnolds will be interred near the graves of Hemingway and his fourth wife Mary on July 21, on what would be the writer's 106th birthday, in the Ketchum Cemetery.

As in life, friends surround Hemingway in death

By John Miller
Associated Press writer

BOISE — Tillie Arnold was working at an Idaho mountain resort back in 1939 when she came across an adventurous writer named Ernest Hemingway, who was at the lodge's restaurant eating marinated herring and drinking a beer for breakfast.

"I burst out laughing and said, 'Mr. Hemingway, is that breakfast?'" Arnold wrote in her 1999 book, "The Idaho Hemingway." "He said, 'Yes, daughter. Have some. It's good for the kidneys.'"

The encounter at the Sun Valley Lodge was the springboard for a relationship that made Arnold part of Hemingway's tight-knit circle of friends — a group that is remaining close even after death.

Arnold, who died in January at the age of 99, will be buried in a plot next to Hemingway's grave on July 21, the author's 106th birthday. The body of Arnold's husband, another

old Hemingway pal who died in 1970, has been dug up from an Iowa graveyard to be placed in the plot in Ketchum next week.

Historians and Hemingway buffs say the burial of Tillie and Lloyd Arnold helps complete the circle of friends Hemingway made during his two-decade relationship with Idaho, where the Nobel Prize-winning writer shot himself to death in 1961 after a career that produced

Please see **HEMINGWAY**, Page A2

A great photo of the Hemingways and Arnolds after a bird hunt

CHAPTER TWO: PART THREE

THE SEND-OFF OF PAPPY AND TILLIE

NDQ **Hemingway:**
Places & People

North Dakota Quarterly   **Winter & Spring 2006**

DAVID NUFFER

The Sendoff of Pappy and Tillie

Driving over Timmerman Hill into Ketchum, Idaho, on that Wednesday afternoon (20 July 2005) opened the memory chest once again to the emotional impact this small mountain community has had on me.

Two people caused that emotion, both now gone, one years before, the other just months ago. One was an icon, the other nearly so: Ernest Hemingway and Tillie Arnold.

Over the course of thirty years I had immersed myself in the lore and legend of Ernest Hemingway and then, 17 years into this consuming spell, Tillie had come into my life. And we, along with my wife, Mary, became friends.

Ernest Hemingway, Tillie Arnold, and Taylor Williams

211

As I passed by familiar landmarks down the main street of town, including Mac's Cabins where Hemingway stayed in 1946 and were known for some years now as Ketchum Korral, my thoughts were of Tillie and her husband who we were burying the next morning at the foot of Hemingway's grave in the Ketchum Cemetery. That was appropriate because they were best friends from 1939 when Hemingway first arrived in Sun Valley, through eight visits to the valley community until the Hemingways moved to Idaho in 1959 before Ernest's death there in 1961.

With Donna Kimbell, Tillie's younger sister, we focused on preparing and guiding the event to a satisfying conclusion. I expected last minute hiccups and was not disappointed. First of all, as presiding pastor at the ceremony, I was to wear a suit and tie, but I left home without a pair of socks. I was prepared to go sockless since I knew Papa and Tillie would not disapprove, but I managed to find a store that morning that sold me some socks. The night before I had met with the videographer at a bar in Hailey, and I'm glad I did because he didn't seem to have a grasp on the significance of this event or any ideas about how to proceed in memorializing it. Everything seemed to be in order as I left him and continued on into Ketchum. The mortician who had practically volunteered his time to assist in the interment ceremony was to meet with me at 9 A.M., an hour and a half before the ceremony. He was fifteen minutes late and he had forgotten to bring the podium. While he called in to retrieve the podium, he unloaded from his station wagon the small square vault which was to hold cremains of Pappy and Tillie Arnold. It was black and scarred as if it had been resting in open storage someplace. No problem, he said, "I'll spray-paint it gold right now." And he did and it was beautiful. During the lead-up to the ceremony he was busy setting up the podium and sound system and training a new employee at the same time. Then the photographer was fifteen minutes late. And the flowers I had ordered and confirmed the day before had not arrived. I am proud to say that I did not anger or panic, and at precisely 10:30 I began the interment proceedings minus only the flowers.

We had no idea who or how many would attend. I had visions of five or six. We set the area with twenty-five chairs and sixty people showed up. It was a perfect group of old friends under the trees planted when Hemingway was buried, now tall and creating bountiful shade on a hot day. A few remaining friends from those earlier days are still alive and they were there including Bud Purdy, rancher, and his wife, Ruth.

The ceremony went perfectly and included opening and closing prayers, a brief description by me of the lives of Pappy and Tillie, and testimonials from Bill Smallwood, Tillie's collaborator on her book, *The Idaho Hemingway*, and Donna Kimbell.

We gather here today to lay to rest Lloyd and Tillie Arnold, together again for the first time in three and one-half decades. This day, July 21, was chosen because it is the 106th birthday of Ernest Hemingway, Lloyd and Tillie's beloved friend. In fact, it was Gene Van Guilder and Lloyd and Tillie Arnold who became Ernest's first friends on his initial visit to Sun Valley in 1939. And it was 44 years ago on July 6 that Lloyd and Tillie stood on this spot as Hemingway was laid to rest here. Now they are all together here in eternal repose.

Lloyd "Pappy" Arnold was hired by Union Pacific in January 1937 as a photographer for Sun Valley. In 1938 he became chief of the department, and Tillie joined him from Council Bluffs, Iowa. Lloyd played a key role with Gene Van Guilder in enticing Hemingway to Sun Valley. (Van Guilder died from accidental shotgun wounds in 1939.) Hemingway arrived with Marty Gellhorn on Sept. 20, 1939, and took over suite 206 in Sun Valley Lodge. On Sept. 21, Hemingway asked Lloyd and Tillie to breakfast, and from that meeting on, Tillie said, "Ours was destined to become a laughing, joking, kidding, teasing, friendly, loving relationship." Hemingway's first son, Jack, expressed his feelings toward Lloyd and Tillie in forewords to each of their books about Hemingway. Lloyd's was titled *High on the Wild with Hemingway* and Tillie's *The Idaho Hemingway*. About Lloyd, Jack said, "Lloyd had a well-founded understanding of the elements which go to make up a sportsman as well as a deep love and appreciation for the sportsman's country." It was Lloyd that led the effort to build the Hemingway Memorial above Trail Creek, and it was Lloyd who once said, "There were never any bad days when he was around." I imagine Ernest would have said the same thing about Pappy and Til.

About Tillie he wrote, "I am convinced that one of the principal charms of Sun Valley that kept my father returning at every opportunity (eight times over 22 years) was the warmth of the welcome and the wonderful coterie of kindred spirits he found there to share his many sporting interests. The spiritual nucleus of that little group of fellow sportsmen was Tillie Arnold. "Not only did Papa find her famously attractive, but she demonstrated that wonderful and unusual combination of loyalty, sound values, and brains which he held in high esteem in his ideal women." Hemingway once said of Tillie, "Fine diamonds are indestructible."

The slow motion aftermath of the funeral left us all in a strange place, both sad and euphoric. Perhaps the absolutely right thing had been done, and Pappy and Tillie were now resting in the place where they belonged. I think we all felt we belonged, for a brief few moments, with the storied and legendary past of these close friends. Burial may signal closure, but, in my mind, it is never enough to end feelings of love.

213

The reception following at Sun Valley Lodge's Sun Room was unflawed. The food presentation was beautiful, the bartenders efficient and friendly. About 35 people attended, and the event closed out the "sendoff" in a proper way.

I was on my own that night and inclined to revisit the past. My perambulations began with a visit to the Hemingway Memorial above Sun Valley Lodge, a simple but moving tribute to the writer built in large part through the efforts of Pappy Arnold. Then a glass of wine or two in the Eddie Duchin Lounge at the Lodge where Hemingway often imbibed. I followed this with a drink or two at a few downtown Ketchum bars that resounded of new generations, then to the Christiana restaurant, all that's left of the Atkinson's motel of the mid-century. It is the place where Hemingway had his last dinner in the corner booth (number 8) before he killed himself the following morning of July 2, 1961. I sat at a table at the bar level and looked out over table 8 on a lower level while thinking about the time Tillie, Mary, and I dined at the next table over from 8 and became close friends.

That morning, at the end of the ceremony, I expressed the essence of the occasion with the words of Hemingway, adapted from his eulogy to Gene Van Guilder written 66 years before: "They have now come home to the hills. They have come back now to rest well in the country they loved through all the seasons."

And then the close, "Thank you for this day, Lord. Amen."

CHAPTER THREE

PATRICK HEMINGWAY

Mouse

When I found myself at the same reception with Hemingway's second son, Patrick, at the Key West home of his childhood, I stayed close by to catch his observations and opinions. And he had many. We were standing on the front lawn at 907 Whitehead Street that January evening in 1985. We were among a crowd of academics and others attending the third annual literary seminar of the Council of Florida Libraries, a four-day event. The subject: Patrick's father. It was titled, fittingly enough, "Hemingway: A Moveable Feast."

I heard Patrick demolish the myth of the plethora of six-toed cats that were supposed to have roamed the property in the '30s. "There were no cats here," he said. Later that night and during the days that followed, he offered other comments, such as these:

* "Key West was one place where Dad lived and was happy. He was here 10 years."
* "By the age of 35, that man had everything."
* "Having captured the earth, he wanted to venture to the stars."
* "The flatness of Key West was made for kids."
* "I loathed fishing, the motion of the boat. Jack [number one son] could never adjust."

The three Hemingway boys. Left to right: Jack, Patrick, and Gregory

In my notebook from the seminar, I described him as "five-feet-nine or -ten, grey slacks dragging on the ground, sports coat too long, glasses case in the breast pocket, striped blue sport shirt, no tie, horn-rimmed glasses, big, gentle laugh, protruding ears."

Contrast this description with one I made 10 years later at his second home alongside the Missouri River in northern Montana:

"Patrick has a round face, straight nose, dark hair with intrusion of grey, black-rimmed glasses, Band-Aids on the back of his left hand and the middle finger of his right hand. He has a straightforward, aggressive, yet gentlemanly demeanor. When he gets into a subject, his voice increases in pitch and sound. He wore a green shirt and a worn, cable-stitched green sweater with a hole in the left arm just below the elbow patch. His pants were pleated brown, with a brown belt."

The latter rounded out a brief description of the man. But there was more to come and much to learn in my three-hour visit in Montana with him and his wife, Carol. But first, about Patrick and his father.

Within the constraints of his professional life and sundry adventures in wars and on the Gulf Stream, Ernest Hemingway managed to be a moderately attentive father. Mouse, as he nicknamed Patrick, became an occasional companion as he grew from Rue Ferou on the Left Bank in Paris to Cuba to the L Bar T Ranch in Wyoming to Africa and Ketchum. Patrick was a cabin boy at eight years of age in 1936 when his father took his cruiser, *Pilar*, to Bimini to fish. He was in Sun Valley, Idaho, in 1940 when Hemingway was there with Martha Gellhorn, his paramour and soon-to-be third wife. He was aboard *Pilar* for one of Ernest's Crook Factory expeditions off Cuba to find submarines during the early years of World War II. In 1945, in Cuba, with his brothers, Jack and Gregory, he visited the Finca Vigia home of Ernest where Mary, his fourth and last wife, presided.

Patrick married Henrietta "Henny" Broyles in 1950. They traveled to Africa where he completed an apprenticeship to a white hunter in Tanganyika in 1955 and became a white hunter himself, making his father very proud. Henny died of diabetes and kidney failure in 1963, and Patrick later married Carol Thompson in the early 1980s.

Some of Hemingway's comments to or about Patrick tell a story of love and pride:

* Adding a modifier to Patrick's name, Ernest once wrote to the five-year-old: "Mexican Mouse, dear old Mex, go easy on the beer and lay off the hard liquor. Blow your nose and turn around three times before going to bed."
* To artist Waldo Peirce: He looks like a "Chinese woodchuck."
* To F. Scott Fitzgerald: He's "built like a brick shithouse."
* To Arnold Gingrich, editor of *Esquire* magazine: "I'm afraid he'll be bowlegged, but that's better than knock-kneed."
* To the mother of Pauline, his second wife and Patrick's mother, in 1934: "Patrick is always about the same, the best companion that I know."

* To his first wife Hadley, in 1940, on his imbroglio with Max Eastman: "Mouse said I should leave it alone and 'let our ancestors fight his ancestors.'"

* To Patrick from the war-torn Hurtgen Forest in November 1944: "Our favorite game is the cow. Today we ate the tenderloin of the tragic cow. A kraut did his best to do away with us, but a man fed on cow cannot lose."

* To white hunter Philip Percival in May 1956: "Thank you for proposing Patrick to the association. I think he will make a good hunter because he shoots very well and is not afraid of anything and has good ability with the language and has a decent personality."

* To "Dearest Moose," in his last letter to Patrick from Ketchum on March 22, 1961: "Things not good here nor about the Finca and am not feeling good but mailing this may make feel better. Kuss, Papa."

A little more than three months later, Hemingway died.

I didn't write in a notebook or use a recorder as I talked with Patrick and Carol. I felt that to do so would be to violate the unwritten "code" of Ernest Hemingway. One of those values, I was sure, was that one does not violate the privacy or confidence of a friend or try to take advantage of a conversation. In any event, it is likely to have curtailed honestly expressed opinions.

So I put my brain in gear, determined to remember as much of our chat as I could. After I left Patrick and Carol at their cabin and drove out of town, I stopped a few miles down the highway and madly scribbled into my notebook everything that I could recall. It's amazing to me to this day how much there was. I had no intention of publishing these observations, but now, more than a decade later, I decided to write a small book about the people I have met who knew Hemingway. Time has its way of wearing off the corners of resolve, especially as increasing amounts of information surface.

The accuracy of this transcript must be considered. After all, it was my memory working; and memories, as we all know, can be faulty. But the essence of this rare conversation with the now only remaining son of Ernest Hemingway should probably surface into the public realm. The prospect of being sued brings no comfort, but here it is.

A Chat with Patrick and Carol Hemingway
Fourth of July 1995

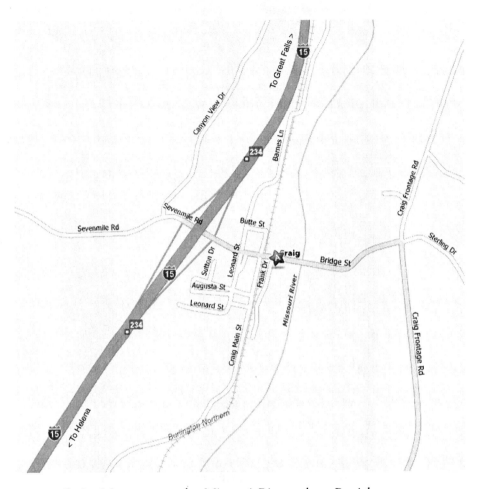

Craig, Montana, on the Missouri River, where Patrick owns a second home

The town of Craig, Montana, is about 40 miles north of Helena, on the banks of the Missouri River, near central Montana's Gates of the Mountains Wilderness Area. On this Independence Day, it consisted of a general store, a bar, and some thirty 30 houses. I turned off the interstate toward the river on the right and took an immediate left down a dirt road that ran parallel to the railroad tracks and the river for a few hundred yards. I was on my way to a visit with Patrick and Carol Hemingway that Tim Larrick, a San Diego friend and husband of a cousin of Carol, had arranged and to which Patrick had graciously agreed. I crossed the tracks and continued northward another 200 yards where Patrick Hemingway awaited at the head of the driveway that led to his "fishing shack."

Sitting on unkempt land on either side of his property were trailers. His cabin was made of wood logs with a front entrance porch and a back porch half-open and half-enclosed, ten yards from the Upper Missouri River. The entryway held a fishing pole rack with eight poles standing in a row. The house had two bedrooms on the south wing, a modern kitchen/living room with a fireplace in the middle of the north wall, and the master bedroom beyond. Pictures on the wall were of ducks and birds in flight. The only book I saw was *A Book on Duck Hunting*. I didn't see a picture or a reminder of Ernest Hemingway anywhere.

I soon learned that Patrick was a passionate man with well-substantiated opinions. He was free with them, but he seemed to check many of them out with Carol to assure himself that everything was okay with what he said. He knew where he was headed and had personal direction. He flew true intellectual colors without arrogance. Adjectives that apply: affable, open, intelligent, resolute, and determined.

Patrick not once referred to Hemingway as Papa. It was always Dad.

We drank a Bozeman-brewed beer on the enclosed back porch for a while and then drove to a clubhouse by the side of Lake Holter nearby for hamburgers. Altogether we talked for about three hours.

On the Hemingway Society and Collectors

Said Patrick, "I have never understood the fascination with typescripts and manuscripts with all the edits. It's what's finally published that counts. A lot of collectors don't care at all about the writing, the literature, just the game of collecting and selling."

On Hemingway's letters, he said, "Everyone knows the person who writes a letter puts himself in the best possible light. Letters are not precise, they are not writing. The academics think the truth is in the letters and it isn't. And they call Dad Ernest as if they knew him." I gathered from these remarks that Patrick held his father's view that letters should not be published.

Patrick and Carol were unhappy with the Hemingway Society over a copyright lawsuit. "It cost us $250,000 to fight this lawsuit. Jack and I [curious omission of Gregory] offered several times to settle but their lawyer, who thought he was going to make a big name for himself, wouldn't settle.

We were forced to take it all the way. The judge, after hearing arguments for five years, finally, I think, grew tired of it all and judged in our favor.

"Now, of course, the society members are as friendly as you please, not the men, the wives." Carol thought their display of friendliness was overreaching.

"In the beginning, they were so friendly and charming. Now I'm out for blood. They're so naïve, they remind me of children playing grown-up games. What they don't understand is business. You don't have anything if you don't have clear title. You have nothing. It's like having property with an easement. They misused Mary's bequest for a foundation to help young novelists into a financial resource for their own research; for example, a grant to Jim Nagel for his book of Agnes Von Kurowski's letters, *not* what Mary had in mind. Von Kurowski was a nurse in Italy who tended Hemingway in a Milan hospital in World War I, and his first love.

"Nagel, Susan Beegel, Bob Lewis. We used to think Allen Josephs was different, but he voted with the others. And Don Junkins. He calls me from Bimini speaking poetically about being where the hotel [Hemingway stayed there] used to be before the hurricane came, the sun splashing down . . . and so on."

The Susan Beegel mentioned here was an academician and editor of the *Hemingway Review*. I asked Patrick about her hemochromatosis theory about his father, but Patrick was having none of that.

I talked about my friend and fellow Hemingway Society member Jim Brasch as someone who understands the intricacies of writing as Hemingway did it. The response I received was dismissive. "The only communication I've had with him is a letter and a phone call." It was not negative, but his lack of enthusiasm could indicate that Brasch has fallen into the society academic cesspool as far as Patrick was concerned.

The society was to meet later that month in Havana, but Patrick had not been informed.

On the End

I reminded Patrick that the next day was 34 years since the burial of his father in Ketchum on July 5, 1961. His response was akin to "no regrets, let's get on with it." But in my opinion, he was as tortured by his father's final act as everyone else who had studied and admired the man.

Referring to the description of Hemingway's last hours in Mary's book, *How it Was,* I remarked that "Mary said that Ernest's last words were, 'Good night, my kitten.'" Patrick was disbelieving. "Who's the source?" Patrick didn't trust Mary's book, especially the description of Hemingway's last day.

I confided that Tillie Arnold believed that Mary had purposely left out the keys to the downstairs room where the guns were kept. I'm sure that was what Patrick suspected. Patrick's response "I think Mary subscribed to the same tenets as Herr Joseph Goebbels" suggested that he agreed.

Stairs leading down from the kitchen to the gun locker. Hemingway walked down these stairs in the early morning of July 2, 1961.

Musing, Patrick said, "Leaving so much of what was important to him behind in Cuba could lead to suicide. He was NOT manic-depressive."

Patrick and Carol were glad no one revealed what happened at Mayo or information on the doctor who prescribed the shock treatments (see chapter seven). "On my last Mayo visit," Patrick said, "he was in a secure ward with barred windows and doors. No question, after the last treatments, he had no choice but suicide.

"When I arrived in Ketchum after he died, George Brown and I went to see the priest. Mary didn't know suicide was no longer unacceptable to the Catholic Church." Brown was an old friend who dined with Ernest and Mary on his last night, July 1, 1961.

According to Patrick, Dr. George Saviers, a Ketchum friend, said to Patrick at the funeral, "He was always crazy anyway." Saviers was not a Patrick favorite. Also at the funeral was Charles Thompson of Key West. "He insisted on being there, said 'I was his best friend,'" Patrick said. I noted that at least several thousand people would make the same claim.

Patrick recalled that someone there asked him, "Is it significant that he died in Ketchum?" Pat responded, "I told him as significant it would be for Thomas Mann to die at O'Hare Airport." Patrick didn't think highly of the Ketchum people that surrounded Ernest there and said that he thought that the place was ruined now. I don't know if this was for him or others or everyone.

On Hotchner

"Hotchner may have been inaccurate in places, but he did a pretty good and sympathetic job. But printing the book, as commercial as it was, was designed to set the record straight. He's generally a pretty good fellow. Mary tried to exclude Hotchner from Dad's story, *The Dangerous Summer*, an impossible task." Hotchner had published a memoir of his friendship with Hemingway, *Papa Hemingway*, in 1966, over protests from Mary Hemingway.

On Androgyny

Patrick spoke eloquently and passionately about Hemingway and his instinctual knowledge. "Dad knew that the great social integrator of the two sexes was sex. He understood sexualism from both sides. A good writer can write from both viewpoints, inside out.

"When Dad had lunch once with Somerset Maugham and another gay writer from Britain, they were no match. Dad dominated the conversation."

On the Key West Years

Patrick told me that he didn't have much interest in his father's career in the late '30s "when our family was breaking up. I didn't understand why he had to leave for Spain. I called *For Whom the Bell Tolls* Dad's Western. But I've kindled an interest in that time period, and *the Bell* is really a good novel.

"By the time Dad was 35, he knew all there was to know about war. And after the Spanish Civil War was over, he was worn out."

Patrick told the story of a man named Peps, who "owned a big piece of wine country in Spain and in later years in Cuba. He had asked for Dad's endorsement to the U.S. Embassy. The embassy came unglued. They showed Dad a picture of Peps receiving the Nazi Iron Cross. When confronted, Peps said, 'Tut-tut, Papa, it was only a ceremonial matter.'" Patrick didn't describe Hemingway's response, or I forgot it, but it's easy to imagine since Ernest was clearly antifascist.

According to Patrick, "The Lincoln Brigade in the Spanish War was very political. They were absolving themselves by sacrificing their lives for their cause, Communism."

Patrick took the blame for what happened to the Key West home. "I sold the property. If I had been smarter, I'd have put in codicils guaranteeing that what has happened there couldn't have. All that foliage and trees weren't there when we lived at 907. And there were no cats. Dad had cats in Cuba, but none in Key West. The only cat on the property was a handicapped one that Dad shot with a .22 because he felt it had been run over and should be put out of its misery."

When Patrick's statement about the cats was reported at the 1985 Council of Florida Libraries meeting in Key West, the next-door neighbor who had owned the shot cat corroborated it because no one believed it. "Hemingway became abusive to animals because of his safaris to Africa," she said.

Patrick didn't seem to have much regard for Toby Bruce, his father's helper for years. Patrick said that Toby couldn't stand the heat of Key West and wanted desperately to leave, but his wife, Betty, wouldn't go. Betty, he said, was the subject of his dad's unpublished short story, "The Key West Girl."

On Sara and Gerald Murphy

Sara and Gerald Murphy were friends from the '20s who lived in Cap d'Antibbes in Southern France and Paris. Patrick said that "Dad learned a lot from Gerald Murphy. It wasn't all bad. Dad adopted from Gerald the use of the word 'daughter' in referring to practically every woman but Mary. This happened naturally as friends began referring to him as Papa."

At a party in New York City, Sara Murphy asked Hemingway, "What do you think of my friends?" Patrick laughed when he repeated his dad's response, "I've never seen so many second-class passengers since I sailed on the Mauritania."

According to Patrick, Gerald Murphy was bisexual and became increasingly neglectful of his sexual duties to Sara, who, in turn, was losing confidence in herself. "So Ada MacLeish, Pauline, and two other literary wives got together and schemed to put Dad and Sara together out on the *Pilar* to restore her self-confidence."

On Literary Matters

Patrick quoted his father: "Revolution is ecstasy but it is continued in tyranny."

Following is my recollection of a small exchange between Patrick and Carol and me:

P   [*Looking at me over the top of his glasses for emphasis*]: Dad was a snob, you know.

C: He wasn't with the jai alai people.

P: That was a different level. Among writers, I mean. I think you have to judge writers against other great writers. Like that California writer.

D: Jack London?

P: Yes.

D: London wrote a lot of bad books.

P: But he wrote some great ones. *Sea Wolf*...

D: *Sea Wolf* was a great book.

Patrick said later in the discussion, "I may have moved to Montana because of Steinbeck's *Travels With Charley*. He said he would live in Montana if it were on the ocean."

Patrick compared writing to quantum mechanics. "Both disciplines are complex and difficult."

Referring to the research Hemingway did for the retreat from Caporetto in *A Farewell to Arms*, he said it came mostly through observation of the Eastern Turks a few years after his ambulance driving experience in Italy during World War I. He recalled an old story his father liked. "When the Turks were fighting the Christians, they captured a Christian general, skinned him, and hung his skin over the Turkish general's headquarters. This drove the Christians into such a frenzy they smashed the Turks for the last time.

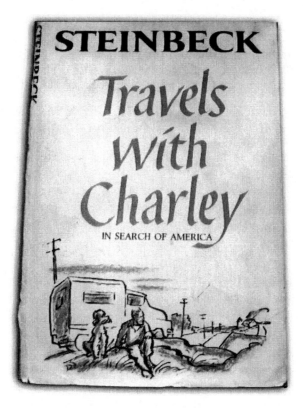

Cover of John Steinbeck's great book Travels With Charley

Then, when the *Pilar* was out hunting U-boats in World War II, Dunabeitia caught an iguana on one of the islands, skinned it, and hung it on the mast of the *Pilar*. This amused Dad."

Patrick also remembered an incident with Andre Malraux, a respected French writer, who visited Hemingway in his suite at the Ritz shortly after the liberation of Paris. He was dressed in full uniform that contrasted to the bootless, shirt-clad Hemingway. Malraux demanded to know how many men he commanded. Hemingway replied, "10 or 12, maybe a few more." Malroux snorted, "Moi, 2,000." I commented that Hemingway would never have asked that question. Patrick continued, "So Dad said, 'Quelle dommage that we did not have the assistance of your force when we took this small town of Paris.'"

Carol pointed out that Malraux became minister of culture for France, thereby forsaking his serious writing for, and I interrupted, "a government job." The Malraux incident is described in Baker's book *Ernest Hemingway: A Life Story* on page 419.

Miscellaneous

Patrick, on charges that Hemingway was a Communist: "There was a continuing joke around our house. Dad always said, 'Water closets of the world unite. You have nothing to lose but your chains.'" This was confirmed by Robert Manning writing in the *Atlantic* magazine in 1965, but in the context of the owner of the Floridita renovating the restroom.

"Jose Garate [see chapter 4] affirmed my belief that Martha was a flirter. I implied that in my introduction to Finca Vigia edition and got an irate letter from Martha saying it wasn't true." Here, Patrick is referring to the Finca Vigia edition of *The Complete Short Stories of Ernest Hemingway*.

"From Dad, I heard the story on Martha. I really heard the story on Martha. But then they were equally self-regarding."

Referring to his younger brother, Gregory, saying almost with a sigh, "Gregory has a lot of self-inflicted wounds."

"Jack should have been in Paris at the Hemingway-Fitzgerald Conference in 1994." Jack is John Hadley Nicanor Hemingway, or "Bumby," Hemingway's first son.

About Carlos Baker's Hemingway biography: "Careless Baker was inaccurate at times, but those that followed weren't close to the whole truth."

Patrick and I both expressed our concerns about what would happen to Finca Vigia if it fell into the wrong hands. "We've had calls," Patrick said.

About his father: "I met him when he returned from World War II, and he was in bad shape. He had bronchitis and was drinking heavily. I think it took him two or three years to get it back."

"Californians are from Arkansas and Oklahoma."

I got the feeling that Mary Hemingway was not one of Patrick's favorites either. With the faintest hint of sarcasm, he referred to her living in New York "as the wife of a great writer should." This did not quite compute to me, as Mary lived in out-of-the-way places in Cuba and Idaho. Also, New York is a good place to be when you are administering a literary estate like Hemingway's.

"Dad was once asked by a journalist if he knew Annie Oakley. He said 'No, but I knew Sarah Bernhardt.'"

"Dad never took notes, but he kept everything."

CHAPTER FOUR

JOSE ANDRES GARATE

Jai Alai, the "Happy Festival"

It was clear that he was born to jai alai when, in a small Basque village in northern Spain, he slapped his first pelota against the wall of the church's courtyard.

His name was Jose Andres Garate, and he was six years old.

Garate won an Olympic gold medal in 1924 at the age of 17 and turned professional that same year. Soon he was known as one of the best pelotaris in the world.

In 1946, he married, and a year later, he helped inaugurate the new Fronton Palacio in Tijuana, Baja California, where he competed until 1954. He retired that year to the stately, old-line community of Mission Hills in San Diego.

Jose's brother Pedro, also a well-known pelotari, retired first and opened a restaurant in Tijuana across from the Fronton at the corner of Calle Siete and Avenida Revolution. He called it Chiki Jai, which means "small party." It was a hangout for the jai alai players, and Hollywood stars such as Robert Taylor and Natalie Wood patronized the place. Pedro operated the restaurant until his death in 1985, but it is still open and thriving until today. For many years, a Christmas card from Ernest and Mary was tacked to the back wall of the restaurant.

When Jose retired, he became a regular at the old San Diego Rowing Club handball courts where he popped nitroglycerine tablets during tournaments to control his chest pains. In 1979, after a quadruple bypass surgery, he gave up handball for tennis.

And that's when I met him. He often played tennis with a friend of mine, Pat Patterson, who knew Garate's history and my interest in Hemingway and so arranged a meeting. From that came an interview in Garate's home on March 28, 1994, 19 months before he died. Through the age apparent on his face, you could see traces of an old magnetism in his smile.

Notes from That Interview

Jose Garate, born in San Sebastian, Spain, and reared in the small town of Villabona in the Basque country, would be 87 years old on April 11, 1994, a few weeks after this interview. He won the gold medal in the 1924 Olympics in Paris for jai alai by defeating a player who was considered to be number one at the sport. He gave the medal to a young lady and never saw it again. However, 68 years later, he returned to the Olympics where he was honored and given a replica. Jose came to Miami in 1924 to play jai alai, then to Shanghai, China, in 1932 to play in the Far East league. He was there until 1939 when the fast-coming World War II forced him back to Miami.

Jose was under contract with Miami in the winters until 1947 but played intermittently during the summers in Havana, Cuba. In the early '40s, Jose and his brother, Pedro, met Ernest Hemingway at the fronton in Havana, Cuba, and were befriended by the writer.

According to Jose, "Hemingway tried jai alai but his hand was too big for the cesta [similar to a glove in baseball]." He liked the players, but he was especially friendly to all anti-Franco people who came to Cuba. Juan Dunabeitia was one of these, and he sometimes lived on Hemingway's fishing boat, *Pilar*. Dunabeitia was big and strong. Hemingway didn't want any sissies around him.

Scott Donaldson, in his highly regarded biography of Hemingway, *By Force of Will*, wrote that "no American writer devoted more time and energy to the world of sport than Ernest Hemingway. Sports are referred to in 43 of his first 49 stories." Donaldson made one passing reference to jai alai in his book, but it wasn't indexed. In fact indexes of the books of top-rung Hemingway biographies have little reference to jai alai, although Hemingway certainly had an interest in the sport in the midforties and continued written contact with some of his acquaintances and friends in the sport for years.

Jose continued, "Felix Areito, playing as Ermua, the name of his village in Spain, was the object of Martha's intentions [Martha Gellhorn, Hemingway's second wife], which did *not* go unnoticed by Papa who was *very* observant. Ermua roomed with me at the Hotel San Luis, and he received phone calls constantly from Martha. Finally, Ermua told Martha to 'go to hell.'" Jose said

Hemingway and jai alai pals at Finca Vigia in the early '40s
From left, bottom row: Ejuibar (nickname, Mickey Mouse),
Miguel _____, Hemingway
Top row: Pedro Garate, Felix Areito or Ermua, Patrick Hemingway,
Jose Garate

he reassured Papa that Ermua respected Papa too much to do anything with Martha. "I have nothing good to say about Martha.

"Later, when Hemingway went to Spain, he gave the keys to the Finca to Ermua, and while we held several parties there, we never touched the wine cellar. This infuriated Papa. One time around the pool at the Finca, Papa and Ermua donned the gloves and boxed. Papa was snapping Ermua's head back when Ermua suddenly landed a big shot flush on Papa's chin. Papa staggered, almost fell forward, recovered, yelled, 'You son of a bitch,' and chased Ermua around the pool.

"Ermua was at one time the second best jai alai player in the world. He was killed in a car crash six years ago [1988]. He was 16 years younger than me.

"I've never heard of La Bodequita del Medio." This supports the notion that, though touted as a favorite hangout of Hemingway and home of one of Papa's supposedly favorite drinks, the mojito, none of it is true.

"I drank with Papa at the Floridita many times and ate oysters with him at Ambos Mundos Hotel. I also fished with him and knew Gregorio, Papa's mate aboard the Pilar. One time, Papa was fishing with a man named Winston Guest, who was the owner of Aerovias Guest Airlines. Papa was drinking from a giant jar. I thought it was water, but it was gin, Gordon's Gin, a Hemingway favorite. He also drank Red Label Scotch. Marquis de Riscal was his favorite red wine.

"He was a great guy. He once said to me, 'If you ever need any help, let me know.'

"I'm positive he would have helped me if I had asked. He was very polite to poor people. He cared about them. He was very loyal and true. He was so kind. I've known a lot of people in my lifetime. I put him number one. He had no pretensions. You would never know he was a famous writer. Whenever we played water polo at the Finca, I always got on Papa's side. He was like a bear. I played tennis too with Papa, in 1943 and '44.

"I was there along with 50 other people at the much-written-about birthday party at the Club Cazadores del Cerro hunting club. Papa sat at the head of the table, with Patrick to his right. Patrick collected all the empty wine bottles. Ermua was seated 15 to 20 yards away, and Papa threw an empty wine bottle at him, which he caught. Then he threw one to Juan (Dunabeitia), who caught his. Then Papa threw one to the Chilean consul, a stocky man with glasses, and it hit him in the middle of his forehead. There was much blood, and Papa felt very bad about it. Papa had to have a good arm to accurately throw those wine bottles 15 to 20 yards.

"I saw Papa drunk many times. Once, along with the earlier bloodied Chilean consul, 15 people visited the Tropicana nightclub in Havana. I had driven to the club with Papa and his chauffeur. In those days, you ordered full bottles of hard liquor, and Papa ordered scotch, gin, and bourbon. We started drinking at 9:00 p.m. and concluded at four the next morning. I was keeping tab on the bottles and paid the bill, after discovering that the establishment had added two bottles to the bill, which I had them remove. Still drinking at the end were Juan Dunabeitia, Pachi Ibarlucia, and Papa.

"Pachi Ibarlucia was strong, brave, and a good fisherman. He was part of Hemingway's Crook Factory, whose mission was to locate and sink German submarines off the coast of Cuba in World War II. He didn't play much jai alai because he wasn't very good. Pachi had two brothers in Havana, Julien, whom Papa called Tarzan, and Domingo. Domingo and Julien owned Centro Vasco, a Basque Club that Papa frequented. Pachi was stabbed to death in Mexico City during a mugging.

"I was also one of the Crook Factory boys along with Dunabeitia, but I only went out two times." When I asked him if he ever saw any submarines, Jose smiled mischievously. He said that the Crook Factory mission was legitimate, but it was also a cover for fishing and drinking.

"Dunabeitia had been a captain in the Spanish navy, and he had a brother who played jai alai. He came from a rich family in Bilbao. He was number one to Papa in the Crook Factory.

"I was in Pamplona in 1959 for the Festival of San Fermin, when Hemingway was there. He wouldn't sleep in Pamplona. I never saw a man go downhill so fast. I am sure that Papa had cancer or cirrhosis of the liver." This is a confirming voice for Tillie Arnold's belief.

I asked Jose if any biographers had ever contacted him. His response: "I loved him too much to tell people about him. Wherever he is now, he would be happy we are talking about him.

"For many years, Papa and Mary sent Virginia and me Christmas cards."

But this interview did not end our relationship. It motivated three San Diego friends and admirers of Hemingway to host "A Celebration of Ernest Hemingway" during the time of the famous Festival of San Fermin and the *encierro*, or running of the bulls, in Pamplona, Spain. The guest of honor: Jose Garate. The site: the Chiki Jai restaurant in Tijuana. Perfect. It took a year of planning, but invitations were mailed a few months before July 12, 1995, to some sixty people we knew would be interested, and on that night, nearly forty folks filled the restaurant. Second son, Patrick Hemingway, sent his regrets and best wishes, saying he loved our invitation. Several journalists attended and reported on the proceedings.

Writers, adventurers and raconteurs are invited
for toasts, antojitos, readings and fellowship in

"A CELEBRATION OF HEMINGWAY"

Wednesday, July 12, 1995, 6 to 9 pm,
at the historic Tijuana restaurant *Chiki Jai*,
corner of *Calle Galeana Seven* and *Avenida Revolución*.

We celebrate July because it is the month of Hemingway's birth, his death and
the Running of the Bulls at Pamploma.

We meet at the *Chiki Jai* because it was the place of his close friends, José and
Pedro Garate, who established the small eatery next to the *Frontón Palacio* in 1946,
as a rendezvous for Spaniards and Jai-Alai players.

We would appreciate a response to our invitation because the restaurant is tiny
and seating is limited.

RSVP at **296-0605**. Dress is informal.

Hosts: Payne Johnson, Tim Larrick, David Nuffer

**World-class Jai-Alai players
surround Ernest Hemingway
in Cuba in the early 1940's.
Pedro & José Garate stand at
upper left and right.**

Directions:
Cross the San Ysidro border, follow the signs to "Centro - Downtown." Stay in left-hand lane and
turn left onto Avenida Madero. Turn right onto Calle Galeana Seven, then immediately turn left into
the parking lot entrance of the Palacio Jai-Alai. The Chiki Jai is across the street, on the corner of
Galeana Seven and Revolución.

Invitation to a festive "Celebration of Ernest Hemingway." The
evening's star was Jose Garate.

Celebration participants. Left to right: David Nuffer with Txistu, a Basque flute; honoree Jose Garate; and Walter Houk, who knew Hemingway well at midcentury

Funeral invitation for Jose. Note his "killer" smile.

Following my introduction, two of the three organizers read selected passages from Hemingway; and Walter Houk, who knew Hemingway in Cuba in the midfifties and who had flown in from Los Angeles for the affair, read the celebrated paean to the Gulf Stream from chapter eight of *Green Hills of Africa*, one of the most lyrical passages in literature. And at 419 words, one of the longest sentences in the work of a man known for the cliché "short, declarative sentence."

Then it was Jose's turn, and he captivated his audience with memories delivered in a voice so soft that it brought a clear silence to the room. "If Papa had been here tonight," he said, "he would have been enchanted. He'd head straight to the bar and order a gin."

Garate said about Hemingway, "He was curious, intelligent, and spoke perfect Spanish. He was open, not a bit of a hypocrite. He didn't like lies. I have never met a better man," and he added, "If I were a woman, I would have been in love with him."

Houk was asked for his thoughts. "Hemingway was such a powerful personality that once you experienced him, you'd never forget it. He was a great big bear of a man, who was very gentle, very kind, beautifully behaved."

To end the evening, a recording of Hemingway's two-minute-ten-second speech made in 1954 on acceptance of the Nobel Prize for Literature was played for the assemblage. It was an uplifting finale to an extraordinary evening of Hemingway-style fun.

A little more than three months later, Jose Garate passed away. He was 88.

As is said in the Basque country of Spain: "Agur. Lurran bego," or "Goodbye old friend, beneath the soil."

CHAPTER FIVE

BETTY BRUCE

A Conch of Key West

Few can claim that they are true Conchs, those born and reared and living in the southernmost of continental U.S. towns, Key West, Florida, one for decades nearly isolated from the rest of the country. Not even Ernest Hemingway could own that title even though he lived there from April 1928 to Christmas 1939. But Betty Marino could.

Her family, all Conchs, owned an appliance repair business in Key West. When she joined forces with T. Otto "Toby" Bruce, she entered the Hemingway circle because Toby (his initials plus a *y*) had become a friend of Hemingway in Piggott, Arkansas, where they shot traps together in the late summer of 1928. The father of Hemingway's second wife, Pauline, lived in Piggott. At that time, Toby was 18 years old, junior to Hemingway by 11 years. Tobs, as Ernest nicknamed him, became the writer's driver, money holder, furniture builder, and anything else needed until Hemingway's death. He was the secret negotiator when Hemingway bought the Finca Vigia in Cuba for $12,500.

Ernest was so impressed with Betty that he wrote a fictionalized piece about her called "A Key West Girl." It wasn't published, but the manuscript can be found at the JFK Library in Boston.

Much later, in October 1958, the Hemingways and Bruces met in Chicago; and from there, Toby drove Ernest to Ketchum, Idaho, while Betty and Mary traveled by plane. The next and last time Toby visited Ketchum was as a mourner at the graveside services for Hemingway on July 5, 1961, three days after he had killed himself. Betty chose not to attend.

Betty Bruce and her husband, Toby, in earlier times

Betty Bruce was a librarian at the Monroe County Public Library, where she was curator for the Hemingway collection, when I first met her in November 1975. She was friendly, obviously wary, but witty in her caution with strangers who had an interest in the writer. It didn't take her long to size me up as a man without a hidden agenda. I just wanted to know how it was to be a friend of the writer. After a short period, she unlocked a small room and led me into her "archives." As I looked through the old photos, she continued to give me her views and insights.

In a letter to Betty that I penned on the plane home, I thanked her and told her that I didn't get a chance to meet Tobs at the Sea Store where he worked, a miss I've regretted ever since. But in trying to express my gratitude for her generosity, I wrote, "Well, I'm out of Conch town now, but not really. I think, like E.H., that you always leave a piece of you behind if you love a place. And always, always the need to come back and see how it's developed, how it's done, that strange piece of yourself that, if you understood it better, you could leave behind in a lot of other places. But that would mean you're a Conch and how many have that privilege?"

That was a bit obtuse, but I understood it and hoped Betty did as she wrote a nice note back to me. As a matter of fact, I did return to Key West three more times, the last in October 1985. And this time, I took notes.

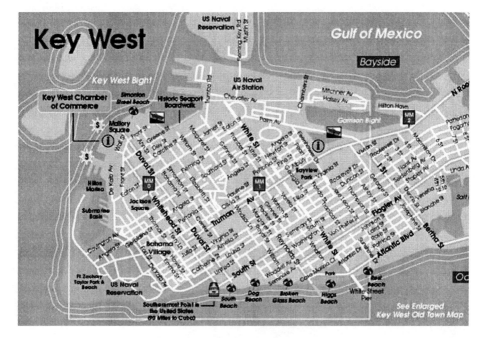

Map of Key West

Monroe County Public Library

700 FLEMING STREET
KEY WEST, FLORIDA

11 December 1975

Mr. David Nuffer
874 Cordova St.
San Diego, CA 92107

Dear David:

Thanks for the nice letter and for the article. Tobs and I both
enjoyed reading about your visit to Sun Valley. Tobs and Charles
Thompson attended the funeral but have not been back since then.

Our young visitor from Sweden is:

Mats Edholm
Hoganasgatan 11C
753 30 Uppsala, Sweden

I am sure he'd be happy to hear from you.

Best regards to you both.

Sincerely,

Betty Bruce
Betty Bruce

Mrs. Betty Bruce
Monroe County Public Library
700 FLEMING STREET
KEY WEST, FLORIDA   33040

MAIL EAR
FOR
CHRISTM

Mr. David Nuffer
874 Cordova St.
San Diego, Ca.
92107

Letter from Betty

Before that though, a meeting bursting with energy and synergy and
feelings—centered about a man of mythic quality—exploded in the hotels
and bars and streets of his former home. It was as if the stars of academe and
their moons had collided with the sun. It was the Third Annual Literary
Seminar sponsored by the Council for Florida Libraries, and for the four

days of this magical event in Key West, January 10-13, 1985, I walked in euphoria among men and women who talked of one thing they knew a lot about, Ernest Hemingway. I had not expected this kind of excitement, and I was thrilled by it. It was much more than professors reading papers; almost all of them summarized their papers in near-spontaneous fashion. Poetry was read, passion was evoked in the meeting chamber (Tennessee Williams Fine Arts Theater), emotion overtook the congregation like an evangelical church service. It seemed that Hemingway himself was guiding the meeting and the evening events with a hidden hand, pushing the buttons, enjoying it all, and loving it.

The Hemingways' home at 907 Whitehead Street, Key West

Charles Scribner the younger was there. So were Bernice Kert, author of *The Hemingway Women*; Michael Reynolds, successor to official biographer Carlos Baker; Allen Josephs, expert on *Hemingway's Spain*; Bob Gadjusek, author of *Hemingway's Paris* and a beloved member of the Hemingway crew; Jim Brasch, chronicler of Hemingway's Cuba library; Donald Junkins, combative and affectionate poet; and Maurice and Marcia Neville, owners of a highly valued Hemingway book collection. All of us formed the Pier House Ernest Hemingway Late Night, Loud Music, Drinking, Dancing, and Discussion Society.

It was too bad that Betty Bruce had fled town to avoid this meeting. She would have thoroughly enjoyed it. On my way from the airport to the Pier House on the day before it started, I'd dropped by the library and left a note from me and one from Nita Jensen Houk, whom I had met late in 1984. Nita had known Betty back in the midfifties when Nita was Hemingway's secretary. My note reflected my call to the meeting coordinator from the Council of Florida Libraries, who told me that Betty was not "participating" in any of the activities. The coordinator said, "Apparently she doesn't want any publicity." I wrote to Betty that I had to laugh, that "the reason you slipped out of town was that you thought it was bad form and that you didn't want the 'pesterment' [Betty's word]."

Nita received a letter later from Betty. She wrote, "I am truly sorry I didn't see David, but I couldn't take the hoopla. I realize there were many sincerely motivated people involved, but I'm tired of trying to explain that Ernest was a very complex man. We had a very pleasant friendship and he was a good friend to us. It doesn't fit the more exotic—wrong word—you understand I am sure—picture so many seek."

Betty then closed the letter lamenting the passing of Tobs the previous May. "He used to say we had more fun accidentally than most people have on purpose." Mrs. Knight, Betty's assistant at the library, told me that he had been "as thin as tissue paper, and just finally gave out." He was 74 years old.

Nine months later, almost to the day on another visit to Key West, a friend and I found Betty at work at the library. It was October 11. When I asked, she said it was okay to take notes. The following are some insights on her outlook on Hemingway matters:

On leaving town when the Hemingway Literary Seminar had been in Key West in January: "I didn't have high enough boots . . . or else my hips were too short."

I asked if she was ever going to write any of it down? "No no, it's all been done. Overdone."

On MacKinlay Kantor: "Mac Kantor was here. He was either from Harvard or Yale. Never could keep those two straight. Someone told me that he was an obnoxious drunk but when I met him he was quiet and courteous. Then we were out for dinner and this loudmouthed jerk was making a lot of noise and it was Kantor. I said we were both right about him." Walter Houk, Nita's husband, was at the Finca in Cuba when MacKinlay Kantor, with his wife and three kids, showed up just before lunch. Betty cooked for 15 that day, and Toby tended bar. Betty was in the kitchen most of the middle part of the day. She had dismissed Hemingway's staff because she couldn't speak

Spanish. Kantor was hardly a model of self-effacement, and even the kids were obnoxious about their "famous" parent until they noticed that brought little response. When the Kantors left early, Hemingway said they probably felt they weren't sufficiently at the center of attention.

On Patrick Hemingway, regarding the imminent death of Lorine Thompson, who, with her husband Charles, had been early friends of Pauline and Ernest in Key West and close to their boys: "Patrick is on my dirt list. He didn't visit Lorine when he was in town [for the January Seminar] and she was lucid then."

On Mary Hemingway: "We called Mary in New York periodically and the last time we talked, she kept insisting that I was a man, that I wasn't Betty. Of course, I do have a very deep voice—too much smoking."

On John Dos Passos: "I'm beginning to like Dos Passos, reading his new biography, although it sure is thick and the type is very small. When he was down here, he came into the room with his big google eyes, and just looked around and left. He was plain rude. There is an old Jamaican saying [on being courteous], 'You talk to people, not cows.' Dos Passos and Ernest had a falling out, but Ernest always had a falling out with other writers."

On a Hemingway fan: "There was this kid who was dying to meet Hemingway, and he begged Toby to arrange a meeting. He came over to our house when Budd Schulberg was there and gave an introductory note to Toby to give to Ernest. He was so full of enthusiasm and so grateful. Toby introduced him to Schulberg. The kid shook his hand, thanked Toby again, and walked out the door. Then, as we watched, he did this incredible double take. He couldn't come back in then, but that double take was worth the price of admission."

Betty asked me, "What did you think of the Samuelson book?" Arnold Samuelson was 20-year-old budding writer that Hemingway took under his wing for nearly a year in 1934. Before I could phrase my wishy-washy answer, she said, "I thought it was terrific." I told her I thought the half on Ernest was terrific.

As we left the library that day, Betty mused, "When people left Toby, he used to say, 'Be bad.'" We told her we would do our best.

Betty retired in November 1985, one month after our visit.

CHAPTER SIX

FRANK ALDRICH

The "Kid" at the Floridita

At the tenth anniversary of the Hemingway Society at the John F. Kennedy Library in Boston in July 1990, several celebrities participated, namely, Jacqueline Kennedy Onassis and authors Norman Mailer and Barnaby Conrad. I was more impressed with Frank N. Aldrich.

Cover of program for the 10th anniversary of the Hemingway Society, July 1990

At the farewell lunch, he sat down next to me and I could sense that he was neither celebrity nor academic. It turned out that he was a retired career bank executive. Although there is no mention of him in any of the literature about Hemingway, he was one of Hemingway's "entourage" in Cuba in the '50s at the famous bar La Florida, which Hemingway nicknamed La Floridita. Frank consumed my interest and attention with his stories. Here are some recollections by "the Kid," as Hemingway called him:

A partial photo of Frank Aldrich, author at his left

When Hemingway would come into the Floridita, it was electric. We addressed him as Mr. Hemingway, never as Papa. The bartenders worshipped him and helped keep intruders at bay. When someone overstepped his bounds, he was crowded out by the quickly forming entourage.

The El Floridita bar, Havana, Cuba

He would go to the end of the bar where his bust was or to the middle of the bar where he could command the entire bar from the back mirror. He would talk to me without moving his head, just talking and commenting from the side of his mouth.

One time, on the eve of the Kid Gavilan-Davey Moore fight, he got into an argument with some U.S. sportswriters. Suddenly he said, "Kid, you take these two, I'm heading outside with the others." He threw me his big watch and left. Nothing happened inside or outside as far as I know. Later I got home and found his watch in my pocket. The next day, trembling, I gave it to the bartender at Floridita. Later on I got a note of thanks from Hemingway.

Often when he was out on the Gulf Stream, he would roll into the Floridita at 5 or 5:30 p.m. One time a relative told a friend of his to call me when he was in Havana. He did so on one Sunday and he wanted to go to Hemingway's bar. I said it was unlikely that Hemingway would be there at 1 p.m. but he showed anyway. The friend was a magician on a cruise ship. Ernest surprised me. He walked in and right over to me. 'Hi, Kid, he said. I introduced him to my companion, telling him that he was a magician. Hem clapped me on the back and said, 'Well, if you can fool him, you can fool the best.' You can imagine how I felt.

Another time, some relatives were down right about the time *Old Man and the Sea* came out. One of the group was a very young woman. Hemingway came in, saw me, and nodded, then saw the girl and beelined it for me. The pretty girl said her father thought the *Old Man* was the best thing ever written. And asked for Hem's autograph for her father. He wrote on the Floridita menu, 'To my good friend—, E. Hemingway.' Then the girl said, 'But my father thinks *Across the River* was really garbage.'

Hemingway paused and said, 'Your father did not have enough background knowledge to appreciate the book, and left.'

Frank told me that he had taken intense exception to an entry that had appeared during the summer of 1967 in the bulletin of the American Club in Miami. The editor had written a negative story about Hemingway titled "Tales of the Havana Club."

Letterhead of the American Club in Miami

The editor said it was based on the "opinions of the majority of a cross section of the Anglo-American community in Cuba." Frank penned an emotional reply to "set the record straight." It was published in the bulletin in August 1967.

Here is Frank's letter:

> In your issue of July 31 . . . you feature the late Ernest Hemingway under a tale of the Havana Club . . . As one who remembers Hemingway as a friend and with great fondness, I feel some answering comment is called for.
>
> You say Hemingway was a loner and usually sat alone at the Floridita bar. A writer perforce has to be a loner to some degree. He must work as an individual to preserve intellectual honesty and must avoid dissipating his key thoughts in idle conversation. Your description, however, does not square fully with the man I observed on so many occasions surrounded by a veritable court of admirers, hangers-on and the curious. That his patience sometimes reached its limits is not surprising, particularly in a person who placed such a high value on individuality and privacy when desired, but those people Hemingway cared about he never failed.
>
> As an insignificant young member of the swirling Havana business community of the early '50s, I occasionally dropped in at the Floridita on Friday evenings after a long and often discouraging week of it. If Hemingway was present, he never failed to have a little time and a few words of encouragement for me and others like myself. It meant much at the time and will never be forgotten.
>
> Your flat statement that Hemingway 'definitely leaned toward the extreme left in politics' is misleading in that it would seem to brand him as a Communist sympathizer. He very much tended to favor the underdog, it is true, but if this is to be the criteria for labeling a man a leaner to the extreme left in this world, I for one am sorry. His performance in two world wars are matters of record as is practically his entire life and nothing indicates that his political views were ever a source of concern to his own government. As a demonstration of Hemingway's flexibility relating to politics or perhaps his disdain for such, you may recall his firm and open defense of Fascist-oriented Ezra Pound when the latter was about as far down on his luck as one can get.
>
> As to Hemingway's appearing on a Castro postage stamp, this hardly came about through the author's making personal application for the honor. Hemingway was well known among the rank and

file of Cubans, and Fidel is not exactly averse to using any name for propaganda purposes. The 'farm at San Pablo' (actually at San Francisco de Paula and not truly a farm) was perhaps not confiscated in the technical legal sense. But it would seem that making the property a national shrine is as complete a takeover as any other we know about. Hemingway did not enjoy living in Castro Cuba any more than you or I did, and he left well ahead of most of us.

In closing I wish to acknowledge my appreciation of the fact that you have called things as you happen to see them, but when you speak of the great antipathy* between Ernest Hemingway and the Havana-Anglo-American community I must say that for many of us it really wasn't that way at all.

Once again, contrary to myth, one of those who knew Hemingway was greatly impressed by his kindnesses.

Frank N. Aldrich
President and Chief
Executive Officer

McLAUGHLIN BANK, N.V.

Wilhelminaplein 14-16
P.O. Box 763
Willemstad, Curacao
Telex: 1083/3302
Tel: 612822 Fax: 612820

Business card of Frank Aldrich

---

*   Walter Houk, who lived in Havana in the mid-50s and knew Hemingway, comments that the American Club of Havana was "composed almost entirely of the American colony business community. In my own view it was deadly dull and I can think of no reason that someone like Hemingway would have been even remotely interested in associating with it. As a result I guess there was some antipathy—but mainly on the members' part, not necessarily on his."

CHAPTER SEVEN

DR. ED RYNEARSON

The End Game

It was in the mid-to late 70s that I met Ed Rynearson. One of my public relations clients produced a three-day press conference for California newspaper food and women's editors, and Rynearson was one of the featured speakers in the field of nutrition. At the time, he was a doctor practicing at the Mayo Clinic in Rochester, Minnesota, and had been there both times when Hemingway visited for diagnosis and treatment. He underwent electroshock treatments from November 30, 1960, through December and into January 1961 and from April through part of June 1961, the month before he killed himself in Ketchum, Idaho.

Dr. Hugh Butt was Hemingway's physician for organic disorders and Dr. Howard Rome was one of the two senior psychiatric consultants. It was Rome who prescribed the now-very-controversial shock treatments at the rate of two a day. Ernest visited the Butt home for Christmas Eve dinner, went target shooting with Butt and his son at an old quarry nearby, and visited Butt's home many times because, as Rynearson noted, "he had full bookshelves."

Thus, when Rynearson said that Hemingway stayed at his house a few days before he returned to Idaho, I concluded that it was the second visit when this happened. Ed had color photographs of Ernest taken during the time he was there.

Rynearson said that Hemingway "was a shell of a man" but that he boxed around the pool with Ed's six-foot-six-inch son and was winning, though Ed

The old entrance to St. Mary's Hospital near the Mayo Clinic in Rochester, Minnesota. In A. E. Hotchner's book *Papa Hemingway*, he tells of Hemingway complaining that "they frisk you and lock the door on you." And Hotchner observed that "one barely noticed the bars on the windows."

thought his son was pulling back. Rynearson would go on walks with Ernest, and the writer would read while he was walking. Rynearson offered to take Ernest to a gun club, but Ernest told him, "Once you've shot 300 of those things in a row, what else is there?"

Hemingway signed all of Ed's first editions of Hemingway's works, including the *Life* magazine issue containing *The Old Man and the Sea*. He remarked that he thought that this was the first time he had ever autographed a magazine. He later reflected that he liked his earlier Nick Adams stories better than anything he had written since.

Ernest didn't touch hard liquor during his stay with the Rynearsons but would drink Lancers wine from its clay bottle.

According to Ed, Dr. Rome was a good man and a good psychiatrist. Ed never asked Rome what Hemingway had said to him, and Rome refused to disclose anything to the press after Hemingway's death. He said, "I don't owe anyone that information." That comment is very disturbing since, in my opinion, the shock treatments prescribed by Dr. Rome led directly to the great writer's suicide on the morning of July 2, 1961.

Of interest here is correspondence related to Hemingway's two visits to the Mayo Clinic. It appears that the drug Ritalin, self-prescribed or prescribed to him by his Cuban doctor, Jose Luis Herrera, combined with Serjasil (Rauwolfia) can cause hypertension and depression.

Following are copies of three letters, never before published and considered by the Mayo Clinic as part of a "closed file."

- To Hemingway from Dr. Hugh Butt, dated January 19, 1961, following Hemingway's first stint at the Mayo

MAYO CLINIC
ROCHESTER, MINNESOTA

CLINICAL SECTION
OF
HUGH R. BUTT, M. D.
JAMES C. CAIN, M. D.
WILLIAM T. FOULK, M. D.
RICHARD J. REITEMEIER, M. D.
JOHN A. HIGGINS, M. D.

JOHN M BERKMAN, M. D.
SENIOR CONSULTANT

January 19, 1961

2-330-587

Mr. Ernest Hemingway
San Francisco
DePaula, Cuba

Dear Mr. Hemingway:

I am very glad to send you a summary of our findings during your examination at the Mayo Clinic. You were admitted here November 30, 1960, having been referred by your physician because of rather marked hypertension. The history you gave was as follows:

1918 - Severe hepatitis while in Italy; good recovery.

1956 - Jaundice noted with dark urine and said to have a large liver with ankle edema. Your local physician thought this was the result of over-indulgence in alcohol.

June, 1960 - Began to notice that following wine with lunch you had difficulty in working in the afternoon. Since this time you also noted continued weight loss in spite of good food intake. You further noticed increased insomnia.

On admission you were found to weigh 175½ pounds, your blood pressure was 160 systolic and 98 diastolic, and your pulse was 80. Physical examination revealed a palpable left lobe of the liver down 6 centimeters with a round edge. It was not hard. There was no flapping tremor; reflexes were normal. The remainder of the physical examination was essentially negative.

Laboratory studies showed a normal urine and a trace of albumin; there was a specific gravity of 1.025. Hemoglobin was 14.7 grams per cent; blood urea was 46 milligrams per cent; fasting true blood sugar was 115 milligrams per cent; the bromsulphalein dye retention test for liver function was 0. Prothrombin time was 23 seconds.

Mr. Ernest Hemingway   Page 2   January 19, 1961

Serum bilirubin direct was negative, indirect 1.0 milligrams per cent;
total proteins were 6.05 grams with 3.44 grams albumin and and a normal
electrophoretic pattern. Serum iron was 167 micrograms per hundred c.c.
and normal. The cephalin cholesterol was negative; the plasma cholesterol
was 182 milligrams; the leukocyte count was 5,300; the differential count
was normal. The blood smear showed the blood cells to be normochromic
and normocytic and the routine flocculation test for syphilis was negative.
Examination of the stool for blood was negative. A repeat of the blood
sugar showed it to be 130 milligrams per cent; for this reason a glucose
tolerance test was done which showed you to be a mild diabetic.

         X-rays of the chest and head were negative. An electrocardio-
graphic tracing showed a rate of 60 sinus rhythm with inverted T in
lead III; V-1 through V-6 were positive T. An electroencephalographic
tracing was within normal limits.

         You were seen in consultation by Dr. R. G. Sprague of the
Metabolic Section who noted the abnormal glucose tolerance test and
thought it indicative of mild diabetes mellitus. He though your present
weight of about 175 pounds was ideal. You were taught the use of the
Tes-tape and instructed in a basal plus 20--2,100 calorie diet for
weight maintenance. He thought that the diabetes was extremely mild
and that you could eat most anything you wish within reason but that
it was important that you keep your weight ideal.

         During your stay in the Hospital your blood pressure was
followed daily and in the early weeks it ranged as high as 220 systolic
and 150 diastolic, but for several weeks now your blood pressure has
been essentially within a normal range of 140 systolic and 80 diastolic
without any hypertensive drugs.

         You were seen in consultation by Dr. J. A. Callahan of the
Cardiology Section and he found no evidence of cardiac enlargement
or damage.

         It is our belief that some of your symptoms might have
resulted from the use of anti-hypertensive drugs and we feel it important
for you not to use these again unless it becomes absolutely necessary.
Funduscopic examination showed many fine vitreous floaters in each eye but
very minimal narrowing and sclerosis of the arterioles and no retinopathy.

Mr. Ernest Hemingway   - 2 -   January 19, 1961

     The presence of a large liver over a number of years with normal liver function plus a mild diabetes made me think that you might possibly have a very rare disease called hemachromatosis. However, I do not feel that this should be investigated further at this time.

     Both Dr. H. P. Rome and I believe that you have made a very good recovery and he will write you in detail concerning suggestions for some drug therapy.

     I do hope that things go well for you. My best regards.

               Sincerely,

               Hugh R. Butt

               Hugh R. Butt, M. D.

HRB:skh

P.S. At the present time I see no reason why you cannot drink wine but not to exceed a liter a day and I would hope less.

               — HRB.

- To Hemingway from Dr. Howard Rome, dated January 21, 1961

Rochester, Minn
Jan 21, 1961

Dear Mr. Hemingway:

Dr. H. R. Butt has described in his report the findings which were obtained on the occasion of your examination here at the Mayo Clinic.

In elaboration of his report may I add the following:

It is my considered opinion that the depression, agitation and tension which characterized your condition upon the examination initially here was a consequence of an untoward reaction to the anti-hypertensive medication you had been given for the control of your elevated blood pressure.

In our experience Serpasil (Rauwolfia) provokes this type of untoward response in a significant number of patients. Indeed it is for this reason that in consultation with members of the Hypertension Service here at the Mayo Clinic that we have recommended the use of other agents routinely.

It seems to me that the sequence of events following your appreciation of these untoward symptoms was accelerated by the use of Ritalin which apparently was prescribed to offset the depression. Thus, as I see it, the situation was compounded.

The prompt response by relatively normotensive findings soon after the institution of treatment in itself provides a clue. Obviously the stress aggrevated by the pharmacological action of these agents fulminated the condition we first witnessed.

The discontinuance of these agents is obviously a prophylactic measure for the future. Dr. Butt agrees that at the present time you do not need any medication to control your blood pressure. If however in future years a modification of this regimen is indicated please bear in mind the sensitivity you have to all Rauwolfia products.

I feel you should continue the use of Lithium mgm 10 regularly as prescribed until you have had the opportunity to return to what for you is a normal tenor of life.

Similarly I suggest the continued use of Tuinal (Amosecobarbital) in doses of 1½ grains at bedtime. Considering the small amount of barbiturate which this represents I would favor doubling the quantity if it should be necessary to insure a good nights' sleep.

It is my judgment that you have fully recovered from this experience and I see no reason to anticipate any further difficulty on this score.

With kind regards

Sincerely

Howard P. Row M.D.

- ## To Mary Hemingway from Dr. Rome, dated November 1, 1961

MAYO CLINIC
ROCHESTER, MINNESOTA
ATLAS 2-2511

SECTION OF PSYCHIATRY
HOWARD P. ROME, M.D.
DAVID A. BOYD, JR., M.D.
MAURICE J. BARRY, JR., M.D.
EDWARD M. LITIN, M.D.
RICHARD M. STEINHILBER, M.D.
SHERVERT H. FRAZIER, M.D.
THOMAS L. BRANNICK, M.D.
JAMES G. DELANO, M.D.
HAROLD R. MARTIN, M.D.

CLINICAL PSYCHOLOGY
JOSEPHINE C. EWERT, M.A.
JOHN S. PEARSON, PH.D.
WENDELL M. SWENSON, PH.D.

November 1, 1961

Dear Mary,

I very much appreciate the opportunity to reply to your
three questions. As you might imagine, I've asked myself the same
questions and thought about this at great length.

Papa and I talked at length about suicide; his father's,
his own musings about it in the past as well as the abortive attempts
he made immediately before his last visit to Rochester. A discussion
of it was threaded through all of our talks beginning the very first
day when I said in explanation of his being placed on the closed
psychiatric unit, that I had arranged for him to be there because I
thought he was sick and therefore unable to see things objectively.

At that time he accounted for his suicidal attempts saying
that it was the only honorable recourse available to him once he
had arranged as well as he could for your future. He was obsessed
with the idea that he could never again meet his obligations and
therefore would be unable to work. The humiliation and chagrin
he felt at this, all but overwhelmed him with agitation, restlessness,
preoccupation with money matters and of course — depression.

It was obvious that he had the classical diagnostic
features of an agitated depression; loss of self-esteem, ideas of
worthlessness, a searing sense of guilt at not having done better by
you, by his family, by his friends, by the myriad people who had
relied upon him. It was this which prompted me to institute electroshock treatment as soon as I did.

As he improved, the intensity of his melancholic preoccupations
lightened proportionately and then the content of his ideas shifted
to a more familiar theme: he was unable to rely upon his lawyers and
his financial advisors were incompetent, etc. etc. At about this time
he spontaneously brought up suicide in another way. He said that I
could trust him; in fact, he pointed out that I had no alternative
but to trust him. In demonstration of this he then pointed out many
ways potentially available to him saying that if he really wanted to
destroy himself there were mirrors of glass, belts, ways in which he
could secrete medications and the rest. It was obvious to me that we

- 2 -

needed to understand each other for, as I pointed out, unless I could trust him and he trust me we had not the beginnings of a means to work effectively. I said I needed his word which would be good enough for me and he said I had it and we formally shook hands to seal the bargain. This led to a long, long series of discussions which dealt with his idea of honor and we covered everything from bull fighting to the payment of gambling debts, from what was honest writing of what you knew at firsthand to how you had to lean over backwards whether you liked it or not to pay taxes.

From that time on virtually he was on his own. He went out almost daily for walks, for swims, for target shooting, for meals, for trips to the Mississippi and was meticulous about announcing his comings and goings to Sister and the nurses. Quite unnecessarily he accounted to them for the money he had in his possession. For example, when I cashed a check for him he painstakingly counted out the money to them — for he had heard there were rules about that in which they were involved.

Our conversations repeatedly got back to the future; what were the pros and cons of a permanent residence in Idaho as against someplace in Europe or even Africa? And stemming from this such discussions as didn't I think his facing up to the treatments was an indication that he was as good now as he ever had been?

The treatments were an ordeal. They are for everyone because of the feeling of loss of control which attends the confused period immediately after recovering consciousness. He talked at length about having to be in control in order to be able to work; not only in control of his memory which troubled him greatly but also to have things done his way. At length we talked about the importance of everything from exercise to bowel movements, from his kind of a daily schedule, to his need to have someplace where he could sink roots even though he was not there more than a short time each year.

The theme of what it meant to feel free came up in many connections. Freedom to him was vital and it ramified in many directions. It underscored the importance of his being in control and accounted for his great annoyance with the induced memory loss. His struggle to see that things were adequately managed led to double checking the nurses' ways of taking blood pressure, eating less than what the dietitians provided and regularly displaying each time the marked wine bottles. It got so that Sister and I would tease him about being the most scrupulous member of the staff to which he would reply with an uncharacteristic absence of humor that if this was the way to be able to get back to where we had no need to be concerned this would be the way he would do it.

- 3 -

        I was completely convinced that the suicidal risk was minimal.
It was this that prompted me to say to you that I felt I had to trust
him, that if he were ever to get back to work which was life for him,
he had to get to it in his way, free of doctors, nurses and all of the
encumbrances which were a perpetual reminder of sickness.

        We had talked about that, too. He never pushed me for a
decision. This as much as anything else leads me to believe that
I was not gulled into a recommendation by him. The advice I gave you,
good or bad, was entirely my own responsibility.

        I had felt that he was being absolutely frank with me;
particularly was I convinced of this when he more freely than ever talked
about his fears. They weren't the usual kind. For the most part they
centered on a deep concern about his doing things the right way. At
great length he pointed out that he had learned early that there are
only two ways possible and that he had trained himself to be intensely
conscious of the small things which are the hallmarks of the right way.

        You asked what more could you have done. . . . I can't see
that you could have done anything more. He often said that he knew
he was a difficult person to live with and that you had somehow or other
acquired the knack. He was especially proud of the fact that you had
been able to share him with what he frequently referred to as that thing
in his head — tapping his forefinger against his temple. I remember
very well in this connection a day when we talked about the need for
his interminably long telephone conversations with you. This brought
us around to the subject of the care and feeding of writers. He was
more eloquent than he had been for a long time in talking about the
good ones and the bad ones he had known and their wives and their women;
what they were looking for and how damn difficult it was to find it.
He talked of his earlier marriages and the frustrations he had caused
unwittingly because of this thing in his head, as he put it. He
contrasted them with you and then re-explained what he had had in mind
in transferring the money to your account just before he came on here.
He wanted you to know in a more tangible way than he could say it
otherwise that he had a real need of you, had tried to say it on many
occasions and most of all when you had left Spain that hectic summer,
but somehow never seemed to be able to get it out so that it sounded
just right.

        I can't see that you could have done anything more. To be
sure he was dependent upon you, we have talked of this, too, before.
Dependent and yet constantly struggling against an admission of it for
fear that it would betray some sort of a weakness. Each time you
tacitly recognized it, especially when it was caricatured by his illness
and attempted to relieve him of unnecessary preoccupation, you will
recall that he insisted that you like all women, tend to overlook
important details. Then he would busy himself with lists only to end

- 4 -

up having you do what he could have done had he not really wanted to rely upon you in the first place.

For weeks we talked about the meaning of his unfounded insistence that if he were legally declared a resident of Idaho he would be broke. When we had all of the factual information which was inescapably clear, it seemed to me that then he came to see that what he was really saying had less to do with money as money and more to do with him as a person with productive assets. When we talked about his writing in a direct and unvarnished way, I came to be convinced not only of his need but also of his desire to get back to work.

This is why I felt his discharge from the hospital was necessary. He was keen to go but as I said, didn't push it, and the decision was mine. Before you came back from Chicago he was enthusiastically involved in sorting his papers and there was an air of expectation to all of the preparations which he undertook with gusto. He talked to a variety of people about various routes, he weighed the pros and cons of flying versus driving; as far as I could see this was hardly the activity of a man bent on suicide.

The core question is what more could or should have been done. Should he have gone to a mental hospital for safeguarding? What more telling signs would one have to have to tell that he had recovered? Thinking about these has led me to the conclusion that I feel sure that had I to do it over again today with the information I had, I would do again as I did then. My hope and intention was to do something for him. I truly felt that the risks were negligible and that he and his future was worth all of them and more besides. I could not, and cannot, see Papa having his life measured out with coffee spoons.

I think I can appreciate what this has meant to you; the whole ghastly, horrible realization of its finality. And all of the endless echoes of why, why, why, why. And the totally unsatisfying answers. This kind of a violent end for a man who we knew to possess the essence of gentleness is an unacceptable paradox. It seems to me that these are some of the reasons why the ceaseless effort to make sense of things which seem not to fit. In my judgement he had recovered sufficiently from his depression to warrant the recommendation I made that he leave the hospital. You accepted this in good faith. I was wrong about the risk and the loss is irreparable for you and me and many others.

I wish that these answers to your questions help you find composure in the head if not in the heart.

Sincerely,

There is much to be read between the lines of these letters. A personal judgment here is that prescribed drugs probably played a larger role than credited, and Dr. Rome probably had a good reason not to "owe anyone that information."

Two relevant comments of interest were offered by subscribers to the Hemingway chat line:

> Steve Paul: "My uncle the psychiatrist once wrote a paper on Hemingway's last ailments for the *Psychiatric Times*, possibly sometime in the late 1980s. This predated my johnny-come-lately Hemingway immersion, and I only just this past weekend saw my uncle for the first time in, say, 20 or 25 years. As I understand it, he diagnosed Hemingway's suffering as stemming from brain damage caused by the two Africa plane crashes, and he lamented the wrong-headed treatment EH later received at the Mayo. The brain damage, he posited, affected EH's memory and ability to write, and it triggered or accelerated or otherwise compounded the depression."

> Alex Cardoni: "Steve, my interest in the subject has taken a different approach, looking at the medication EH took over the last decade of his life, especially Reserpine, an often-prescribed antihypertensive agent in the 1950s. At higher dosage, the drug can control hypomanic and manic behavior, but also can produce profound depressions. This was well known in the medical community in the '50s. I think the agent contributed to EH's worsening depression that required hospitalizations and ECT at Mayo, which eventually induced mini-psychoses that Papa could not tolerate, and he ended it all. There were other psychotropic medications available to help control Papa's hypomania, which would not induce/worsen his depressions. And Reserpine, used at low dose for hypertension, has less risk of inducing depressions. All this is summarized in my paper published in *North Dakota Quarterly*, 1998."

Dr. Rynearson died on November 27, 2007, at the age of 86 years.

CHAPTER EIGHT

MARY HEMINGWAY

Miss Mary

A dubious Mary Hemingway and Fidel in a return visit to Cuba after Ernest died.

I never met Mary Hemingway and never expected to. But we did write a few letters to each other over a five-year period in the 1970s. I pried my way onto her correspondence list with a personal reminiscence about my pilgrimage to Ernest's burial site in Ketchum, Idaho, in the summer of 1972. I was wide-eyed in disbelief when her response appeared in my mailbox.

The following is my reminiscence followed by her letter:

KETCHUM, 1972

I purposely avoided thinking about it. My feelings in the end, my thoughts, had to be spontaneous. I had to have that. He would have plenty of reasons to think I was a jerk anyway—whoring as a person doing public relations, as he would put it. But I would have spontaneity going for me, and he would have to respect that while detesting my purpose.

It's hard not to think about how you're going to feel when you've thought about doing a thing for many months. So you have to set your mind to it, write a code to live by in your head. Even though it's artificial, you have to believe it's right. If you do that, your subconscious has it and can do with it what it wants.

The closer you get to the thing you're trying not to think about, the harder it gets to avoid thinking about it, so to trick your mind, you think on the periphery of it—how the roads are, are the mountains green or brown at this time of year, what does the center of town look like.

Driving through Nevada was easy because it is so unlike Hemingway country. Spain would come closest to Nevada, but even it has many hills, many more trees and more mountains and more rivers. California before it was easy too. Hemingway never got to know California well.

Ketchum was smaller than I expected, so it didn't take long for us to traverse it and check out the motels. Our entire family made the trip: Mary, my wife, and our three kids, all teenagers. I picked Swank's Motel because it felt right. The lady at the desk let me know right away that cabin 6, where she was putting us, was the cabin Hemingway used to write in back when McDonald owned the lodge and it was called Mac's Cabins. She said even the fixtures were Hemingway's choices and that he had a door cut connecting units five and six. I chose to believe that.

Mary and I took a short walk through town, and it was easy to see why Hemingway loved Ketchum and the fuzzy, soft mountains surrounding it. There was intermittent rain, and a light breeze brought it to the ground at an angle. So instead of walking to the cemetery, we drove.

The rain had stopped as we stepped over the chain guarding the entrance and walked down the asphalt pathway that ran through the center of the place, looking for what we knew was a "simple marker." I noted the dates on the headstones and could tell which way to go.

Hemingway's simple marker turned out to be a large marble slab set back from the pathway. It lay between two pine trees, one two feet taller than the other. I didn't remember the trees from the picture of the graveside ceremony that appeared in *Life* magazine, so I figured that Mary must have had them planted soon after. At the head of the slab was a small wooden cross that needed painting. It shouldn't have been there. The two trees are enough of God. Just beyond the large marble slab were the graves of Ray and Edna Mark, and it seemed strange that their inscriptions faced Hemingway's plot instead of their own.

If you wanted to pick a place to be buried, you couldn't pick better than the Ketchum Cemetery. Green grass covers the entire area, and it has an unplanned small-town look. It does have a chain-link fence around it, which also is unnecessary since it fights with the harmony of the place with the hills.

I didn't allow myself to think about all the things I wanted to think about because I wanted to save that for the memorial. I did find it hard to swallow as we walked back to the car.

Tomorrow, I told myself, I'll get a bottle of Chateauneuf du Pape and spend my time alone at the memorial before bringing the family to see it.

The memorial should be seen in the sun, I thought to myself, on this 24th morning of June. So I was disappointed when the bright morning clouded up. But at least it didn't fill the sky, so there were spots of sun from time to time.

Some people were in the parking area when I arrived, so I sat and waited for them to leave. Not only should the memorial be seen in the sun, it should also be seen alone. I had played it right so far, and fat ladies with cameras and kids were not going to interfere.

I sat on the wooden fence at the roadside entrance and waited, but as one group left, another arrived. Hell, I had forgotten it was Saturday. By chance, the last group on its way out was led by a man who introduced himself as Joe Clement. He had a happy, weathered quarter-moon face. He'd built the memorial, he said, as well as most cemetery markers in the area, including Hemingway's.

"I noticed a couple of headstones in the cemetery with Clement on them," I said.

"Yeah, those are two of my kids. But I've got five more," Joe said and smiled.

I offered Joe and his companions swigs from the bottle, and a few accepted. Then Joe, on an impulse, walked down to the memorial with me.

"Hemingway could be arrogant at times," he said, "but he surely loved this place. It was hell building it. Christ, I couldn't touch one blade of grass or weed or anything, and it's not easy to carry all my equipment and the stones down and not hurt anything. Hell, it'll grow back."

The sculpture of Hemingway's head was done "by a fella in New York," he said; and then, as the wind picked up, he left and I was alone. A small stream ran between the sitting area and the memorial, which sat atop a long slope down to Trail Creek.

Suddenly, the rain came, and a strong wind whipped through the cottonwoods, shoving them in all directions. It was a violent five minutes that reminded me of the old Hollywood horror movies when the wind would rattle the shutters of the old house just before the murder. Then it snowed a little. This would have been very unusual for summertime, so it's possible that I incorrectly identified cottonwood blossoms as snow. It was very dark as I sat beside the stream with my back to the monument and my coat collar turned up. When the sun reappeared, I would turn and take in the full force of the memorial.

And it came and touched the sculpture of his head, and it shone golden and serene. And I thought maybe, just maybe, what I had experienced in the past few minutes was the light and dark force that was Hemingway.

I'd been saving the last chapter of *A Moveable Feast* so I could read it there, alone. I finished it and began to let my mind wander over all the things that he had written that had so shaped me. Jake Barnes and Bill Gorton and running with the bulls in Pamplona, which I had done, and Harry Morgan and his incredible wife. And then the people who said that Hemingway was a male sexist and didn't understand women and how that was bullshit. And about Nick Adams and Littless and the crippled major whose wife had died. And Francis McComber and Tom Hudson and the Floridita and that beautiful scene there. And about "Sea Change," and "Now I Lay Me," and about "It was like saying goodbye to a statue. After a while I went out and left the hospital and walked back to the hotel in the rain." And about the colonel and the countess and the maitre d' hotel.

And about Carlos Baker writing that Hemingway divided the whole world into two kinds of people, good guys and jerks, and how right that philosophy was and how I would hope that he would put me into the "good" category.

And then I thought about those last tormented days and how no one would ever really know the why and the how of it and how it really wasn't important. And what Hemingway might say if he could talk to me now. So I invented a dialogue:

"Well, Mr. Hemingway, it's clouding up again, and I'm almost out of wine, so I'll be leaving soon."

"Boy, I think I understand what you're doing here, and it's flattering, but what do you really know about me?"

"Not much, I guess, except that I have tried to get inside your skin, and I truly like you and the things you wrote and the way you lived."

"Have you fished and hunted and skied the way I fished and hunted and skied?"

"No, sir."

"Have you accepted great risks to find out about things like war and death?"

"No."

"Have you been poor?"

"Yes."

"And now you want to write a book, just one, a good book, one that will say what you believe life is all about and that it's about man's love for man and how life is very funny if you look at it the right way?"

"That's right."

"Do it is my advice, but remember, it will require changes in your habits."

"I understand that."

"One more thing. Go after the pompous, the phony, the supercilious bastards of this world. Put words in their mouths that you've heard them say."

"I'll try."

"And don't forget me."

I walked down along the stream and found a log lying across it and crossed over and made my way back carefully to the memorial. The sculpture was better than it looked from the other side. His eyes were too hollow, but maybe that's the way they were in the last days. I looked at the river down below, listened to it for a while, finished off the wine, and walked back to the car.

P. O. BOX 555

KETCHUM, IDAHO 83340

9 - 6 - 1972

Dear David Nuffer -
　　　　I'm sorry to have delayed so long to acknowledge your July 5th note and your story about Ketchum and Ernest, which I find very moving, especially the conversation between you two.

　　　　It's of no importance, but the woman at what used to be MacDonald's cabins was inaccurate, saying Ernest had chosen the fixtures and had a door cut connecting 5 and 6. There wasn't any door cut when we were there - 1946 and again in 1947, but that property has changed hands several times since then. Anybody could have cut the door, and somebody added those front porches.

　　　　I planted two sets of trees which died for lack of water. The last set I had transplanted from near the house here and had them watered enough so that they caught on. The local veterans outfit stuck in the cross which, I agree, E. doesn't need. But I don't want to hurt them over such a detail. The river below the memorial plot is Trail Creek, not the Big Wood.

　　　　Best luck with your work.

Mary Hemingway

　　　Today is the first day since July 10th I've had a chance to get at my desk.

Mary's response to "Ketchum 1972"

Two years later, the local newspaper's books editor asked me to review a new biography, *Hemingway in Spain*, by Jose Luis Castillo-Puche. I sent a copy of the review to Mary and again she replied.

This was followed in 1976 by my impressions of another pilgrimage, this time to places in Europe where Papa had lived and written, and she sent back her comments.

Mary's autobiography appeared in 1976. It was impressive, and I wrote a laudatory review for the local paper. However, *Time* magazine, for which Mary had worked as a journalist, didn't agree. I wrote a letter to *Time*, blasting the reviewer. *Time* replied, and I riposted. I sent Mary a copy of my review and the correspondence between *Time* and me. I added a more explicatory summation. When she replied, she expressed opinions of my review and my argument with *Time*.*

In 1981, Carlos Baker, the official Hemingway biographer, published *Ernest Hemingway: Selected Letters, 1917-1961*, despite Ernest's request that his personal letters never be printed. I sent my unflattering evaluation of the book to Mary where she lived in a penthouse apartment in New York City overlooking Central Park.

Our small "correspondence discrete" then ended abruptly. She didn't respond. The Hemingway's lawyer did. He coldly informed me that "Mrs. Hemingway is no longer in correspondence." And that was it.

I was disappointed, but not saddened. As far as I was concerned, I had stepped onto hallowed ground when the wife of a man whom I considered to be nearly Godlike had shown such generosity of spirit with me. She had been responsive, corrective, friendly, revealing and, well, respectful. I had gained a spot of credibility, and I am grateful still.

Mary Hemingway died on November 26, 1986. She was 78 and had outlived Ernest by 25 years.**

---

*   In her response, she revealed in two short sentences her link with Pauline, Papa's second wife (1927-1940) and mother of sons Patrick and Gregory: "Pauline and I became friends when Patrick grew desperately ill at the Finca, and she came (from Key West) to help nurse him. She was also a smart brain and a generous friend to me."

**   In 1977, in New York City Mary was visited by Delores and James Brasch. Brasch is a Hemingway scholar and coauthor of the definitive book about Hemingway's library at Finca Vigia in Cuba. He said later that she was so alive, so dedicated. "She wore skintight clothes and as she talked about Ernest with such enthusiasm, we saw her nipples harden. She was so vital." Brasch said, "I don't know what happened to her but it happened very quickly." When Brasch had heard that she was drinking too much, including gin and milks in the morning, and that she wasn't eating, he called Hemingway's publisher, Charles Scribner, who sent someone up to her apartment. She told Brasch in the early 1980s that she had "three goons" to watch over her.

Ernest receives a congratulatory kiss from Mary upon notification
of receiving the Nobel Prize for Literature.

* * *

Following now is a written record of my correspondence with Mary,
including photographs of her notes to me. The inference is clear from these
letters that whatever difficulties they had as married partners, Mary did
indeed love Ernest.

* * *

Nita Jensen Houk, Ernest's secretary and typist for three years at midcentury,
had an unsatisfactory phone conversation with Mary in June 1985. It was 8:30
p.m. in New York and Mary had just gone to bed. She sounded very weak and
disoriented. There were lapses in the conversation. Mary thought Nita was in
New York. Nita wondered if Mary was under heavy medication and if that,
coupled with her normal drinking habits, it was not helping her. Another time,
Mary called at 1:30 a.m., New York time. Nita's husband, Walter, took the call
and noted that Mary was unusually slow in grasping what he was saying and
he had to repeat things.

October 1, 1974

Dear Mary Hemingway,

The local morning newspaper asked me to review
Castillo-Puche's book (I think I have become San Diego
resident E.H. expert) and I thought you might be
interested in it. I don't know if you agree with my
assessment but I think you do. The book review
editor at the paper sliced a few grafs so I'm sending
along the original too.

David Nuffer
874 Cordova St.
San Diego, CA

Another About Papa

E-D   THE SAN DIEGO UNION   Sunday, September 29, 1974

HEMINGWAY IN SPAIN, by Jose Luis Castillo-Puche, Doubleday & Co., 367 pages, $10.95.

A book has been written about nearly every place Ernest Hemingway set foot or lived. Most have come from university presses. This one comes from Doubleday and is a translation of a Spanish novelist and newspaper reporter who wrote it more than seven years ago. (Carlos Baker's official biography of Hemingway has no mention of Castillo-Puche.)

It is a personal reminiscence. His thesis is to be expected: everything Hemingway was stretched back to his emotional involvement with Spain and, more specifically, the bullfight.

The book, somewhat jumpy in execution, follows the author on a nine-day odyssey to all the old places after he had gotten word that Hemingway had died "accidentally" in Ketchum, Idaho. Castillo-Puche knows that the man has killed himself and most of the book is an attempt at justification, condemnation, and understanding of it.

There is a moving account of Hemingway's visit to the deathbed and funeral of Pio Baroja, noted Spanish novelist and Hemingway influence. There is a curious dissection of the "inaccuracies" in "For Whom the Bell Tolls." If Castillo-Puche's perception is right, there is also the awful truth of the Nobelist's role in the "public relations" of Antonio Ordonez, matador, who gained fame later here in the sixties for fighting small bulls with shaved horns.

The author knew Hemingway only in his fading years, when he was sick and despondent. By the time the reader finishes the book he feels the same way.

In the end you feel somehow repelled at yourself for looking into a man this way. You know why Hemingway would have greeted this book and all the others like it with scorn. — David Nuffer

Letter to Mary with my review of Castillo-Puche's biography of Hemingway, October 1, 1974

P. O. Box 555 - Ketchum, Idaho - 83340

10-5-'74

Dear David Nuffer, —

Thank you for the review which I find fine and dandy. José Luis is a nice guy, but apparently couldn't resist joining the scavenger birds.

I haven't gone back to count in my diaries, but he may have seen Ernest parts of 10 days in all. A lesson to us all in how to blow balloons.

Besto —

Mary Hemingway

Mary's response, October 5, 1974

July 21, 1976
(Ernest's birthday - 1899)

Dear Mary Hemingway,

For what it's worth department:

I thought I'd solved a minor literary puzzle
last month at Hotel Taube in Schruns. Herr Nels, who
rightly relies on his ability to run an excellent
hotel rather than the reputation of his father's
famous guest, decided I was worth trusting and he
showed me the guest register that included the months
of 1926. It was very clear who the "pilot fish" was (A Moveable Feast)
and "the rich": Dos Passos and the Murphys. There
was E.H.'s signature and an address written by someone
else, probably Hadley, for 4 Place de la Concorde, Paris,
followed by Chez Guaranty Trust Co. of New York.
Hadley then signed her name and that of "John Hadley
Nicanor Hemingway (Bumbie) 2 yahre, 5 monat." It had
all been speculation, I believed, about who the "pilot
fish" and "the rich" were. Then, this morning I consulted
Baker and it was clear who they were although no mention
was made of the Taube guest register. So much for my
detective skills.
        Earlier I met Claude Decobert, barman at the Ritz.
He was a quiet, lovely man incontrol of everything at
all times. He said he had met E.H. in 1947 when he
was 17 and that E.H. had taken him/shooting pigeon at
Issy les Moulineaux. And I have to quote the rest (which
I hurriedly scribbled down after I had left the Ritz):

        "He ask me one time if I shoot. I told him yes.
He invited me to his room. He was just back from Africa.
He had 12 guns laid out on the bed. Elephant gun, duck
gun, lion gun...He ask me which one I would use and like
best. I told him the Browning 12. Later he came in
with the gun in a box and gave it to me. He say, 'Every
man must have a gun to defend himself. Don't ever - you
must promise me - never sell this gun. Unless you need the
money. Pass it on to someone young. We must always
look out for the young.' I still have the gun."

        Claude also said that he thought E.H. was a "shy man
and I don't think he drank up to his reputation."
        When I asked Claude if he had read Gigi's book, he

2

said no, that he couldn't read English very well,
but that Gregory had been in the Ritz checking out
facts. The next day I brought in my copy of the book
and gave it to him. He wasn't overly pleased but I
didn't know if that was because he couldn't read English
or because he had heard about the book and didn't want to
read it. I told him I thought it was the best yet,
until yours comes out in the fall. Anyway, he accepted
it (what else can you do?).

So, as we drove into Pamplona on the day of the
opening of the fiesta, following a day full of hard
driving to reach our beds in Espinal, a few kilometers
from Burguete, and in a deluge, and I saw the familiar
gangs of joy-clicking youth and heard the high octave
music from the Txistus, I couldn't help but think
that there are no longer new worlds to conquer; there
are only old worlds to re-conquer. Perhaps that is why
we took the road from Burguete south to Aoiz to Pamplona
on the day before we left for Madrid. E.H. had said
that the pionics took place up the Irati River above
Aoiz and that he had found a place that he didn't want
to describe for fear that the next time he came there
would be 50 cars or jeeps around it. In that episode
he didn't say that the river was no longer the Irati,
but the Urrobi, but I figured that out and chose as
the place a soft meadow, a dirt road through it and the
same beech trees, all at kilometer 52. We didn't stop
there though. Instead, we crossed the old, car-width,
stone bridge at Aoiz and opened our wine at a sheltered
spot south of it and talked of the old days.

Such is the talk of romantic old fools.

Cordially, and happy birthday to Ernest. We still
hear the message,

David Nuffer and Gang
874 Cordova St.
San Diego, CA 92107

Letter to Mary regarding 1976 visit to places where Ernest lived
and worked, July 21, 1976

Mary's response, September 14, 1976

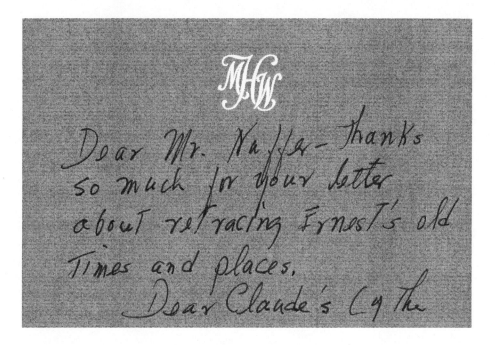

Ritz) memory betrays
him, in one respect. He may
have met Ernest for the first
time in 1947 when he was
chasseur (errand-boy) for the
Ritz's rue Cambon bars. But
Ernest was not then just back
from Africa, to which he
went for the first time in the
fall-winter of 1933-34, and
the second time in 1953-54.
      I can't imagine why we
should have had so many guns
at the Ritz in 1947, and
surmise that Claude was
remembering 1953. E. had a
couple of heavy guns on

that safari; but never shot
an elephant — Never wished
To do so.
It's impossible, of course,
To keep all records straight, or
all memories accurate. this
is just for your information.
Best wishes –
14th, Sept. 1976   Mary Hemingway

E-6   THE SAN DIEGO UNION   Sunday, November 28, 1976

Mary Hemingway's Story

She Was More Than His Wife

HOW IT WAS, by Mary Welsh Hemingway, Alfred A. Knopf, 537 pages, $12.50.

This is Mary Welsh Hemingway's book, and please remember the middle name.

Irish Independence shines from every page. And it does so in bright description of a life that, until Ernest, was as adventurous as his.

She, too, knew of wilderness life and Indians where she grew up in Bemidji, Minn. She fought her way into journalism, badgered the London Daily Express into hiring her, covered Chamberlain and Hitler in Munich in 1938, lived through Hitler's blitz of London, became a Time correspondent, knew her share of the great names including Julian Huxley, H. G. Wells, Ed Murrow, William Saroyan, and she married twice before Ernest.

Enter Ernest through an introduction by Irwin Shaw in 1944 in London, and two adventurous lives joined. "I had been an entity," she writes later, "now I was an appendage." And still later she says, "He had become the most important part of me."

Adjectives are few in this book. Described events do the telling of the people involved, though some names and incidents deserve further explanation. There is no gossip. It is up to the reader to fill in the spaces. And it is all much like (she would not likely say) her husband's writing.

But through it all comes a revealing portrait of the man who influenced so many.

He was ornery, lovable, considerate, inconsiderate, hard-drinking (he made friends with bartenders wherev-

Ernest and Mary Welsh Hemingway in 1957.

er he went), ingratiating, haranguing, witty, magnetic. For the first time, in full force, the legend becomes a human being.

The end has been told before, but never so poignantly, especially the last words between them on the evening of July 1, 1961, when, in preparing for bed, they sang portions of an old Italian folk song and then what was to be a farewell, an old familiar endearment.

"Good night, my kitten," he said.

David Nuffer

My review of Mary's book How It Was, November 29, 1976

Penthouse
27 East 65th Street
New York 10021

2-21-1977

United States 13c

David Nuffer, Esq.
874 Cordova street
San Diego, Calof.
92107

Mary's response, February 21, 1977

In 300 words, you did a
generous, perceptive *MHW* 2-21-1977
job, I thought.

Dear David Nuffer — Do excuse,
if you can, my ridiculous delay in
answering your letters of 19, Oct.
and 29, Nov. I've been away
from here "plugging" the book

almost constantly since Oct.
1st., and hoping to devote decent
attention to your letters, shoved
them under unpaid bills, unanswered
invitations etc.

Thanks so much for your letter
to _Time_. Mr. Maddock must be
either too young for his job, ill-
educated, or unable to read
the language. A snotty, amusing
fellow.

Pauline and I became friends
when Patrick grew desperately ill at
the Finca, and she came over to help
nurse him. She was a smart brain
and a generous friend to me.

About Latin-Am. versions of

Spanish life, they seemed to me to absorb the superficialities rather than the essences. I may be mistaken.

I hope to get back to work fairly soon on the rest of the E. H. mss. But give me time, man, I've been too busy for too long. Please excuse handwriting— I'm tired of the typewriter. Bests— Maxy

END PAPERS

ITEM ONE: TORONTO STAR TYPEWRITER

Unexpected Discovery

When numero uno Hemingway biographer Michael Reynolds delivered his closing remarks at the Fourth International Hemingway Conference,[*] he made a call for action to fill in some of the gaps in Hemingway research. One need, he said, was a precise description of Hemingway's typewriters and "where they are."

He said this on July 11, 1990. Three days later, two Hemingway aficionados, in a cluttered second-floor storage room in an old house on Harboard Avenue, Toronto, typed a statement for historical evidence on an Underwood typewriter used by Ernest Hemingway when he was a reporter for the *Toronto Star*, September 10, 1923, until January 1, 1924.

How this happened calls for explanation.

The two men who typed the statement were James D. Brasch, then a professor of English at McMaster University in Hamilton, Ontario, and myself. Jim and a fellow McMaster professor, Joseph Sigman, had researched and published, in 1981, the first composite record of books in Hemingway's Cuba library—more than 7,000. I first met Jim at a Modern Literature Association meeting in New York City after he had delivered what I considered a groundbreaking analysis of the correspondence between Hemingway and

---

[*] Celebrating both the tenth anniversary of the formation of the Hemingway Society and the dedication of the Hemingway Room, home of the Hemingway Collection at the Kennedy Library, Boston, July 7-11, 1990.

Malcolm Cowley. This fortuitous meeting was followed a few years later by a rather "wet" conference on Hemingway in Key West, Florida. Jim, his wife Delores, and I, and later my wife, became "friends of mutual interest." The friendship deepened over the years.

My wife, Mary, and I visited Jim and Delores at their home in Burlington near Toronto after the Boston Hemingway Conference. During that visit, Jim surprised and delighted me when he told me that Hemingway's *Toronto Star* typewriter had resurfaced, and he knew where it was. The next day we took the train into Toronto.

Jim had secured permission from the owner of the typewriter for us to see it. He was Niel Wright of Wright Realty who had handled the sale of the estate of a Mary Lowry Ross, a fellow reporter of Hemingway's on the *Star*. After prowling through her attic, Wright somehow had gained possession of the typewriter found there, reconditioned it, and stored it above his office in Toronto.

Jim's research was scientifically inconclusive, but he was certain that he had discovered the "lost typewriter." When Hemingway had departed Canada in January 1924, the typewriter was too heavy to carry, so he gave it to a fellow reporter, Mary Lowry. Reportedly, Lowry was the only fellow journalist to see Hemingway off when he returned to Paris. Tillie Arnold, who became a friend of Hemingway 16 years later in Sun Valley, Idaho, said she couldn't imagine the man handing over a typewriter he used all the time. "He was a very generous man with his money when he had it, but not with things that he used."

There was an unfounded, and unlikely, rumor that he proposed to Mary.

Mary Lowry Ross died in the mid-80s.

The statement we pecked out on the Underwood was sent shortly after by Jim to the curator of the Hemingway Collection at the JFK Library.**

** In a pleasant two-for-one, Jim and I found the apartment house at 1599 Bathhurst Street, where Hemingway and the pregnant Hadley lived during their few months in Toronto.

McMASTER UNIVERSITY
Department of English, Chester New Hall 321
1280 Main Street West
Hamilton, Ontario   L8S 4L9
Telephone: 525-9140 ext. 4491; FAX (416) 527-0100

July 14, 1990

To whom it may concern:

This is an imprint of the Underwood typewriter owned by Ernest
Hemingway while he worked at the Toronto Star from 1920-23.
When he left Toronto he gave the typewriter to Mary Lowry Ross
also a writer for the Star. The typewriter was purchased appar₤
ently from the United Typewriter Co in Toronto.

1234567890-/?£½¾¢.?   ""#$%_&'()/

The quick brown fox jumped over the lazy dog.

THE QUICK BROWN FOX JUMPED OVER THE LAZY DOG.

This imprint made with the permission of the present owner, Niel
Wright of Wright Reality, 94 Harbord Ave, Toronto by James D
Brasch and David Nuffer on July 14, 1990.

                                    James D. Brasch
                                    Department of English
                                    McMaster University
                                    Hamilton, Canada

                                    David Nuffer
                                    874 Cordova Street
                                    San Diego, California

Statement typed on Hemingway's Toronto Star typewriter and sent
to the Hemingway Collection at John F. Kennedy Library in Boston

The apartment house where Hemingways lived in Toronto in 1923

The plaque on the outside wall. It says that Hemingway lived there in 1923-24.

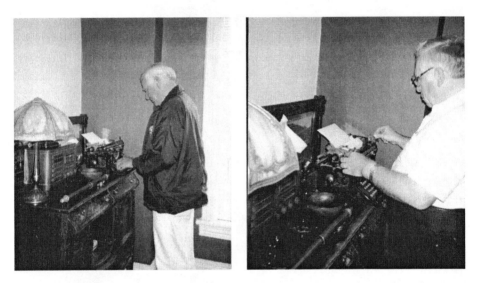

The two Hemingway sleuths at the Underwood keyboard: David
Nuffer and Dr. James Brasch.

ITEM TWO: CAPTAIN REECE DAMPF

Hemingway and the Hurtgen Forest

Captain Reece Dampf and wife

"Mr. Hemingway and Bill Walton, another newspaperman, came to see me one night. Mr. Hemingway had four canteens of bourbon and scotch which, after receiving our orders for the next day, we soon did away with."

These words came from a letter of reminiscences written by Capt. Reece Dampf, a veteran of some of the fiercest fighting in World War II, in the Hurtgen Forest. One of the recipients of the letter was his nephew Ken Dampf, a member of my small coterie of friends when we were growing up in a small desert town in California.

Here are some excerpts:

"After cleaning up Paris, we came under the command of Colonel C. T. 'Buck' Lanham and headed north for Brussels . . . After the first week in November, we moved north into the woods of the Hurtgen Forest, an area of about 350,000 acres of timber . . . We fought in the Hurtgen for 18 days and nights, and our losses were terrible . . . After Thanksgiving, we took a German headquarters bunker about 800 meters west of Groshaus."

It was there that Capt. Dampf first met Hemingway who provided the "hooch" for that night. He wrote that Hemingway thought the war would be over by Christmas.

"Later, when I became executive officer, I would see him at regimental headquarters with the battalion commanders for orders or 'routines' that Buck Lanham used to hand out. After the orders were given, things quieted down, and Hemingway would join in on the bull sessions.

"After the Battle of the Bulge was over, Mr. Hemingway went to Paris and rented a place and invited all officers of the regiment to be his guest whenever we came to Paris on leave . . . When the war was over and he had returned to Cuba, he insisted that he would love to have any 22nd regiment officer as his guest anytime in Cuba. Some did visit him, and they were treated royally."

Later in the letter, Dampf wrote, "I feel Hemingway's death was a great personal tragedy to me. He loved the soldiers and a lot of other people."

ITEM THREE: HERB SAUL

Paris and Hemingway

"Oh c'mon, Herman, get off it!" she said to her always-joking brother. But it wasn't Herman. It was Ernest Hemingway calling to tell her that her husband Herb Saul was okay and working well in Paris. The time was after the Allies had taken Paris in World War II, and Herb was assigned there as a correspondent for an American newspaper.

When Herb and I became business friends in the 1960s, he was an editor for an electronics trade magazine published out of New York. I was trying to persuade him to print news of the electronics company I worked for. When Herb learned of my interest in Hemingway, he told me of the "big drinking parties at the Hotel Scribe," the headquarters for the news media during the war. Hemingway was a correspondent for *Collier's* magazine at the time. He said that Hemingway "was always dominant" at these soirees. "He never talked about himself. He was a very earthy guy, had no pretenses, no standing on ceremony."

Hemingway offered to call Herb's wife when he got back to the States, and that night, when the phone rang and the man on the other end of the line identified himself, it was not surprising that she didn't believe him.

Herb had always been amazed that the writer had delivered on his promise and was very grateful that he did. His wife, meanwhile, was dumbfounded by the gesture and never forgot it—once she recovered.

ITEM FOUR: WILLIAM JOHNSON

A Dissenting Vote

In July 1985, I met for the second time at a party in San Diego a retired writer named William Johnson. He had been a former bureau chief for *Time* magazine in Mexico City, a college professor and author of *Heroic Mexico*, one of the best English-language books on the Mexican Revolution that tore the country apart in the early 1900s.

In addition to having met B. Traven, the author of *Treasure of Sierra Madre*, in Mexico City, Johnson claimed that he was really the one who introduced Hemingway to Mary Welsh in London during World War II. According to Carlos Baker, it was Irwin Shaw who made the introduction at the end of May 1944 at the White Tower restaurant in Soho. I'm not sure if it was that same night or later that Johnson told me he was drinking in the early-morning hours with Hemingway and that Ernest was drinking heavily and wanted people to listen to him. At about 3:00 a.m., Johnson talked Ernest into knocking on Mary's door at her penthouse apartment on 31 Grosvenor Street, which he did. Then Johnson said he went to bed. Presumably, Ernest spent the night, thus beginning the affair that ended in marriage in 1946.

Johnson's opinion of Hemingway was affected by his observation that Ernest was a boring drunk.

It's my opinion that Ernest may have been experiencing what most men do around the age of 44, namely, a crisis of self. There is evidence that he was erratic in behavior during that time in London, so he indeed could have been a boring drunk. I believe that Johnson should have taken a broader view, but then, they were, at that time, competing chroniclers of the war.

ITEM FIVE: THE AUTHOR

A Personal Postscript

H.R. Stoneback, author of *Reading Hemingway's the Sun Also Rises*, a true tour de force of academic enquiry, wrote that travelers often visit the places of Ernest Hemingway. Landscapes and sites "depicted by Hemingway, perhaps more so than any other writer, seem to compel readers to visit the actual places. Many have written of such travels, creating a kind of sub-genre of Hemingwayana." That description certainly applies to me.

In Hemingway's Footsteps

EUROPE

Germany

* Drove through the Black Forest where Hemingway fished in the early '20s

France

* Cap d'Antibes, near Nice: Overnighted in the hotel where the Hemingways stayed when visiting the Murphys in 1924

* Paris: Visited approximately 50 homes, bars, parks, cafes, hotels, including the floor landing of Ernest and Hadley's fifth-floor apartment at 74 rue du Cardinal Lemoine.
* Normandy: Visited the D-Day beaches, Mont-Saint-Michel, Rambouillet, and eight other places he negotiated during World War II

Austria

* Schruns: Stayed at Hotel Taube and visited the room where he stayed (no. 6), accepted the generosity of the hotel owner, Herr Nels, son of the owner when Hemingway was there, who allowed me to look through the hotel register with its historic entries by the Murphys and John Dos Passos; drove up to the Madlener House on top of the pass at the edge of the continental divide

Spain

* Pamplona: In 1960, picnicked on the banks of the Irati River as Hemingway did in 1959; drove up to Burguete north of Pamplona and the Burguete Hotel (*The Sun Also Rises*); drank countless carafes of vino tinto at the Txoko Bar, where Hemingway and his "mob" stationed themselves nearly every day at the 1959 feria; saw the hotel that was Montoya's Hotel in *The Sun Also Rises*, Hemingway's statue near the bullring, several bullfights; and visited other places and ran in the *encierro* three straight days
* Madrid: Drank at Cicotte's, the Hotel Suecia Bar, ate at Casa Botin, strolled down Calle Jeronimo, saw a bullfight at Plaza Monumental
* Granada: Visited Hotel Inglaterra, where Hemingway stayed
* Seville: Walked around the Maestranza bullring, saw a bullfight there
* Santiago de Compostela: As Hemingway did, visited the terminus of the Christian pilgrimage honoring St. James, the church were his bones rest
* Coruña La Coruña: Visited this northwestern city where Ernest and Pauline spent part of their honeymoon in 1927 and the bar, I surmised, that they patronized on the corner of the plaza

* San Sebastian: Walked along the promenade bordering the bay as Jake Barnes did following the Festival of San Fermin in *The Sun Also Rises*

Italy

* Venice: Consumed bellinis at Harry's Bar and gin at the Gritti Palace Hotel, visited the island of Torcello and Locanda Cipriani, plus the room where Hemingway edited *Across the River and into the Trees*

Cuba

* Havana: Visited nine Hemingway-related sites, including the famed Floridita bar and restaurant, the Ambos Mundos Hotel, and Club Nautico
* Cojimar: Walked the site of *The Old Man and the Sea*, the pavilion or templete and bust dedicated to Hemingway, drank at La Terraza Bar, visited the home of Gregorio Fuentes, Hemingway's mate aboard the *Pilar*
* San Francisco de Paula: Strolled the grounds of Finca Vigia, Hemingway's home, and viewed its interior, the guest house, and the tower

Canada

* Toronto: Located with Professor Jim Brasch the typewriter Hemingway used during his time with the *Star*, visited his and Hadley's apartment

USA

California
* Los Angeles: For "research" purposes, patronized the Biltmore Hotel bar, downtown, as did Hemingway

Florida
* Key West: Located 1111 South Street and two other domiciles that he and Pauline rented; toured their 907 Whitehead home, which

they owned; drank at Sloppy Joe's and its previous incarnation, Captain Tony's; drove to the place on the bridge at the next key where he met Charles Thompson, his African safari partner in *Green Hills of Africa*, and other places

Illinois
* Chicago: Watched several games at Wrigley Field
* Oak Park: Toured this suburb immediately west of Chicago, including the place of his birth at 339 N. Oak Park Avenue, the Hemingway museum, his family home at 600 N. Kenilworth, the World War I memorial in the Central Plaza that includes Hemingway's name, Oak Park High School, Oak Park Library, and First United Church of Oak Park where Ernest was baptized

Idaho
* Ketchum, Sun Valley: Paid homage at Ernest's and Mary's grave sites in the Ketchum cemetery and at the memorial east of Sun Valley Lodge several times; toured the Topping House, the last and only home they owned there, Mac's Cabins (now Ketchum Korral) where they stayed in 1946, the downtown bars, the Christiana Restaurant where he had his last meal, Sun Valley Lodge room 206, where he wrote portions of *For Whom the Bell Tolls*, Trail Creek Cabin, the party site, Silver Creek Valley, Picabo, and other places

Kansas
* Kansas City: Visited Union Station that reporter Hemingway covered for the *Kansas City Star* in 1917 and '18, probed and discovered the bathtub near the press room in the Hotel Muehlebach at Baltimore and 12th where Hemingway slept one night with towels for a mattress. I laid down in the bathtub, no towels.

Michigan
* Charlevois: Toured this pleasant Upper Michigan town, a frequent destination of Hemingway's and where he lived in a two-story house one summer after returning home from World War I

* Horton Bay: Purchased a beer at the Horton Bay store, walked around the tiny village, saw where Hemingway and Hadley were married, drove past the Hemingway home called Windemere on the east side of Walloon Lake, and saw the nearby site of the short story "Indian Camp"

New York
* New York City: Conducted research at Dempsey's Bar where Hemingway cracked a cane over his head, which is now framed and hanging on the wall; tipped a few at Algonquin Hotel Bar, Club 21, the Oak Room at the Plaza Hotel, and Toots Shor's; attended a game at Yankee Stadium

Wyoming
* Sheridan: Toured and dined at Buffalo Bill Cody's Hotel, located the home of the Fontans of the short story "Wine of Wyoming"

My Mementos

When I visited Key West in 1976, the back patio had recently been replaced at Hemingways' home at 907 Whitehead. I picked up one of the old bricks, which the caretaker let me take. My adopted brick is large—9 by 3 ¼ inches—with "BALTIMORE BLOCK W.P.B. CO." stamped on it. Ersatz bricks are sold today as souvenirs at the house, but mine is authentic.

Generous gifts to me from Nita and Walter Houk (see chapter 1) included a fossilized seashell Hemingway had bestowed upon Nita and a signature of the man, himself.

In 1991, I was in Horton Bay, at the site of the pier and pier house used by Hemingway in his story "Up in Michigan," the one Gertrude Stein called "inaccrochable." The structures had been demolished in a recent storm, but I found a remnant, a six-inch piece of wood with two nails in it. It now rests on my shelf of first editions.

A decade or so ago, I located two used 1947 Royal portable typewriters and purchased them both. One very much like them, perhaps even identical, is on display at Hemingway's Finca Vigia outside of Havana. I believe mine are of the same genre. One now decorates my office at work and the other, still serviceable, lies on the bookcase in our bedroom.